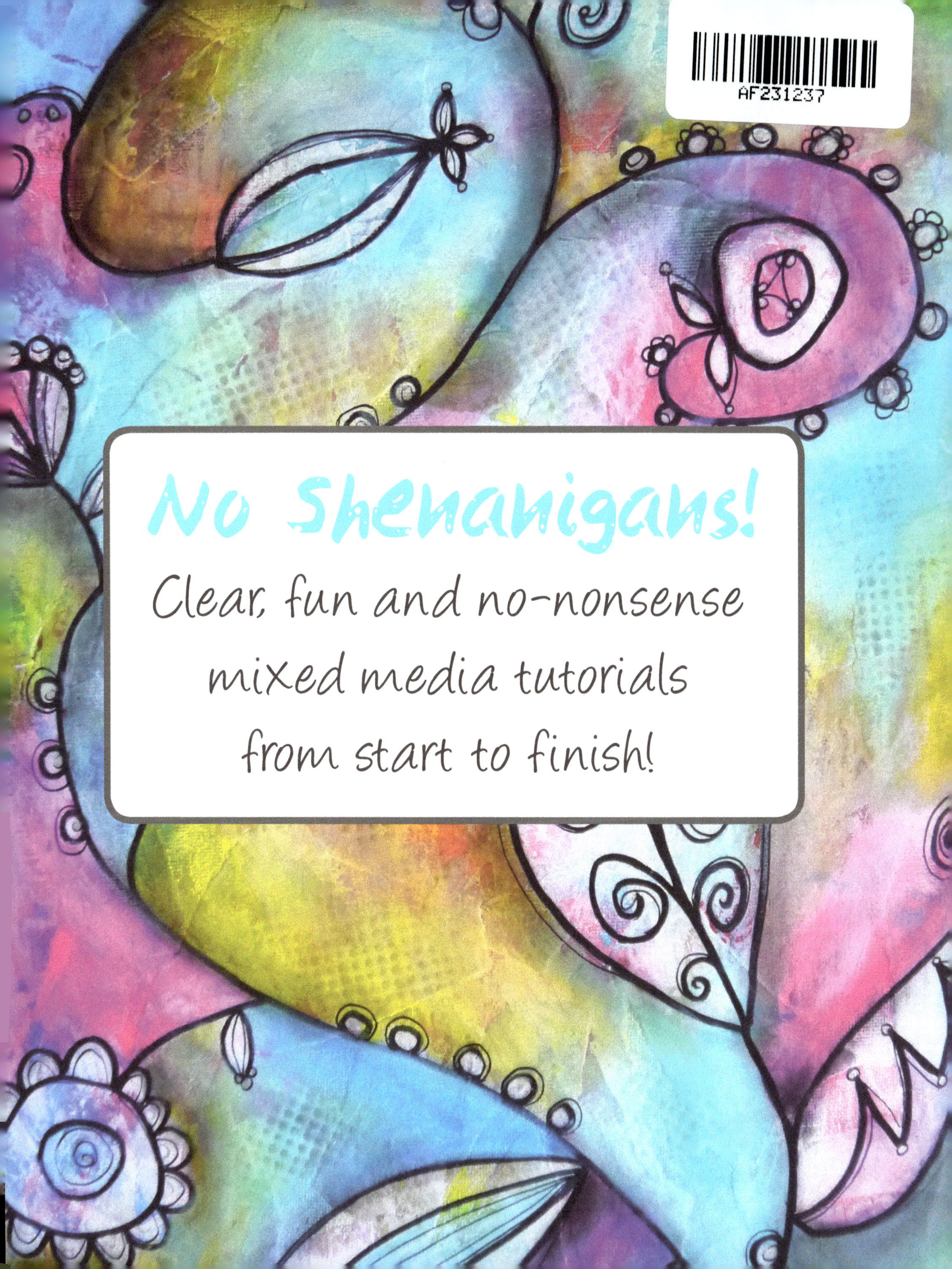
AF231237
No Shenanigans!
Clear, fun and no-nonsense
mixed media tutorials
from start to finish!

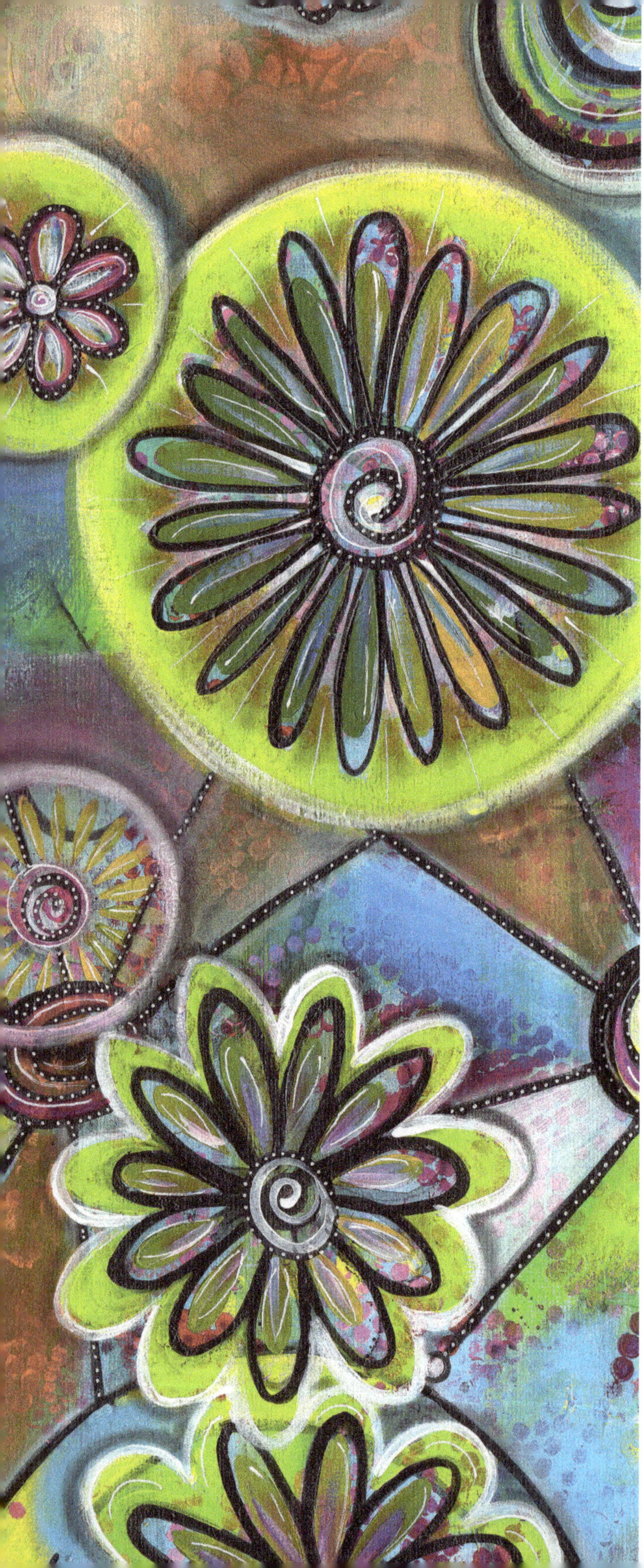

The boring, but important, disclaimer!

Mimi Bondi (Muriel Moret) is the copyright owner for all aspects of this book including artworks, text, graphic design and photographs.

Under Copyright Law it is fair use to reproduce those artworks for personal or educational purposes provided that the notice *"Inspired by the work of Muriel Moret - mimibondi.com"* is attached to the reproduction.

No reproduction may be made of any of the artworks from this book, videos or online content for commercial use (for any reason) without first receiving written permission from Mimi Bondi (Muriel Moret).

If you are unsure about anything related to the above, simply send an e-mail to: **hello@mimibondi.com**

Thank you...

Now go and create something awesome!!!

Aqua Blue
PUBLISHING

Aqua Blue Publishing
A.B.N. 642 148 89 370
aquabluepublishing.com

# Contents



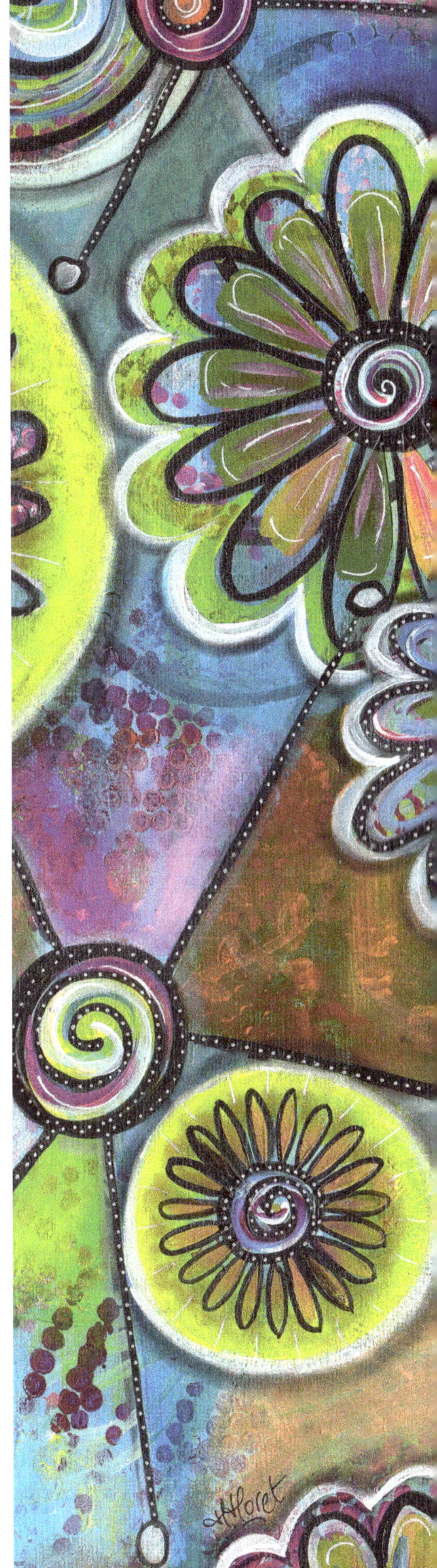

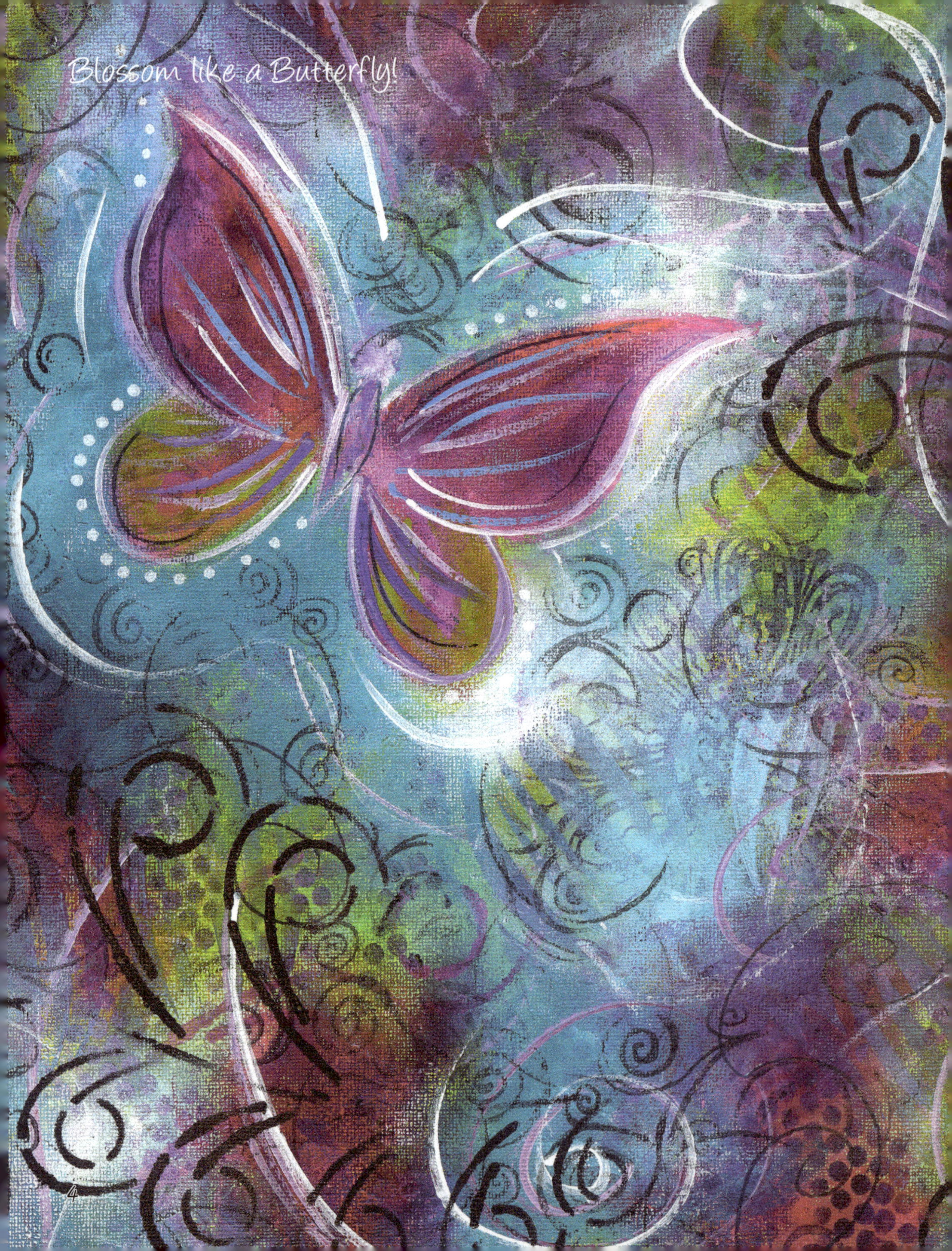
Blossom like a Butterfly!

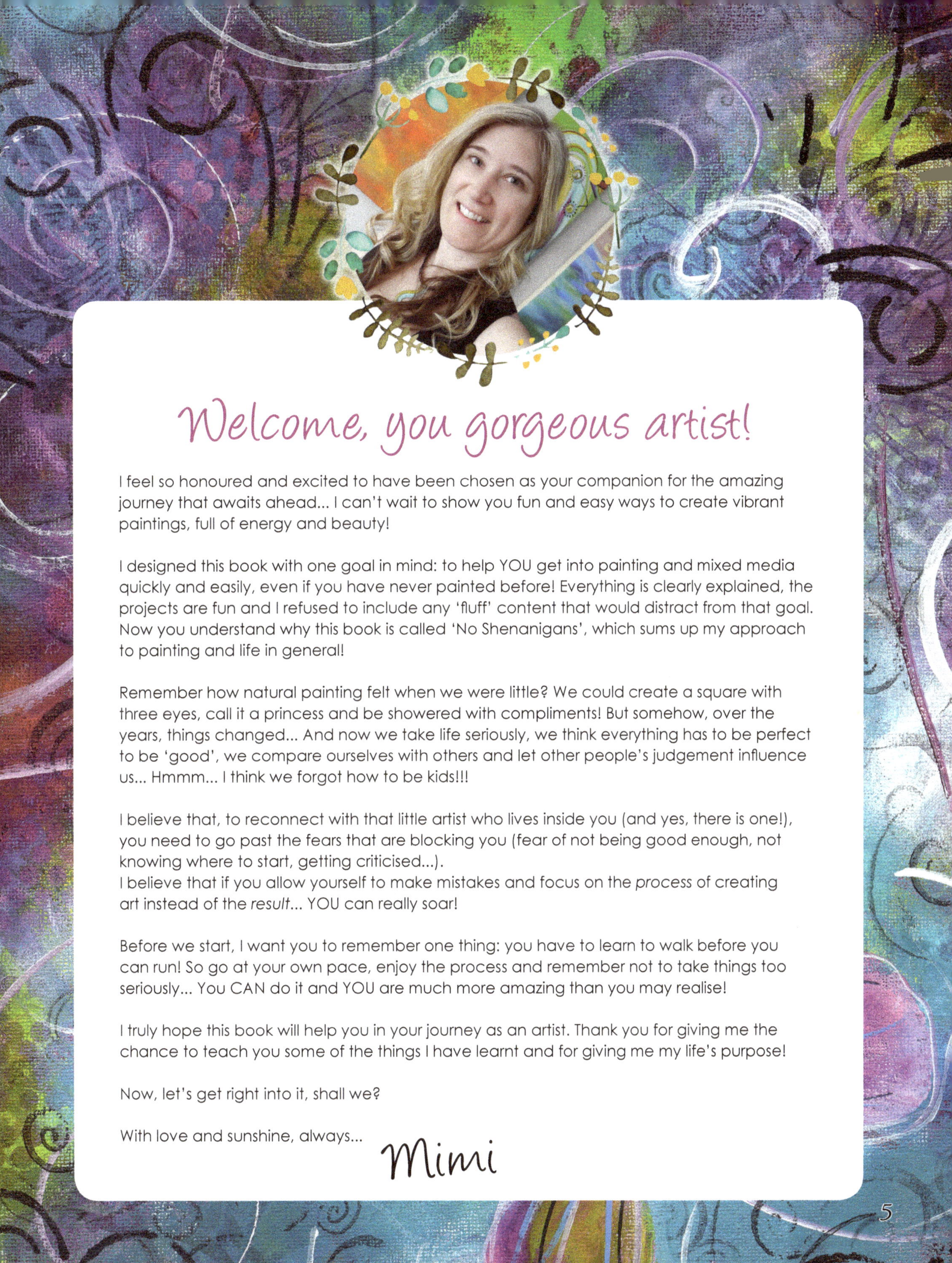

# Welcome, you gorgeous artist!

I feel so honoured and excited to have been chosen as your companion for the amazing journey that awaits ahead... I can't wait to show you fun and easy ways to create vibrant paintings, full of energy and beauty!

I designed this book with one goal in mind: to help YOU get into painting and mixed media quickly and easily, even if you have never painted before! Everything is clearly explained, the projects are fun and I refused to include any 'fluff' content that would distract from that goal. Now you understand why this book is called 'No Shenanigans', which sums up my approach to painting and life in general!

Remember how natural painting felt when we were little? We could create a square with three eyes, call it a princess and be showered with compliments! But somehow, over the years, things changed... And now we take life seriously, we think everything has to be perfect to be 'good', we compare ourselves with others and let other people's judgement influence us... Hmmm... I think we forgot how to be kids!!!

I believe that, to reconnect with that little artist who lives inside you (and yes, there is one!), you need to go past the fears that are blocking you (fear of not being good enough, not knowing where to start, getting criticised...).
I believe that if you allow yourself to make mistakes and focus on the *process* of creating art instead of the *result*... YOU can really soar!

Before we start, I want you to remember one thing: you have to learn to walk before you can run! So go at your own pace, enjoy the process and remember not to take things too seriously... You CAN do it and YOU are much more amazing than you may realise!

I truly hope this book will help you in your journey as an artist. Thank you for giving me the chance to teach you some of the things I have learnt and for giving me my life's purpose!

Now, let's get right into it, shall we?

With love and sunshine, always...

Mimi

# Before we jump in...

## Some things to keep in mind...

Although 'mixed media art' refers to using various visual art media in one artwork, it doesn't mean you have to go overboard! Simply combining layers of paint and adding some doodles with a pen will create a 'mixed media' piece!

With all the supplies available out there, it is very easy to feel overwhelmed...
I recommend you start with just a few essential supplies and add to them when you feel more confident, or if you find a medium you really love. I will therefore focus on what you will need to create all the projects in this book and will explain how I use them as we go along. I believe you will learn a lot faster by using the supplies rather than reading about them!

## Which surface should you use?

Asking yourself what you want to do with the art once it is finished should point you in the right direction...
- If you want to hang the art on your wall: choose a canvas,
- If you just want to experiment, and keep your art private: paint in a large art journal,
- If you are unsure, then I suggest an acrylic paper pad.
Pads are inexpensive and may feel less intimidating than a canvas.
If things don't turn out the way you thought, you can throw away the sheet of paper or paint over it. But if your painting looks awesome, you can still frame it and hang it on your wall!

The projects in this book are mostly done on canvas but that is just my preference. I encourage you to use the surface that you feel most comfortable with for now as the results will be similar no matter which one you use.
As for size, I recommend a canvas, paper pad or journal page approximately A3/30x40cm or 12x18in (big enough so you can really loosen up and experiment freely).

## Which tools will you need?

**Paint brushes**
Although we are going to do a lot of finger painting, I recommend a couple of brushes to start with:  a square 3/4 in (2cm) wash brush and a fine tip brush (size 8 for example) are my favourite tools. I prefer Taklon bristles (soft, long lasting and inexpensive) and plastic handles (because wood quickly falls apart if you 'forget' your brushes in water - artists can get lazy!).

**Small sponges**
These are great for applying acrylic paint with or without a stencil. You can use inexpensive makeup latex/foam sponges or cut a synthetic kitchen sponge in small pieces.

**Mark-making objects**
Here is where you can use your imagination: small plastic cups/bottle caps/toilet rolls create easy
circles, old credit/store cards make great lines and can be used to spread paint... Collect bits of
corrugated cardboard, bubble wrap and anything that could create interesting marks or texture!

## Which supplies to get first?

**Acrylic paint**
Acrylic paints are so versatile, fast-drying, forgiving and easy to find that they should be the first
thing on your list! But, you don't need to buy expensive artist grade paints (yet!) or every single
colour available to start on your journey as an artist...
I recommend getting all the colours you love the most first, as well as some black and white.
My favourite ones (and the ones used the most in this book) are yellow, orange, red, magenta,
purple, turquoise, lime green and white. But, if you can't afford much at the moment, remember
than yellow+red will give you orange and that turquoise+magenta will give you purple so...
Experiment and be creative!

**Metallic and iridescent acrylic paints**
Most brands have a few metallic or iridescent colours in their range but my favourite ones by far
are from the Pébéo Studio Acrylics range. They are quality paints with intense colours that are just
magical! Imagine what these iridescent colours could add to your paintings: Orange Yellow, Red
Blue, Violet Blue, Blue Green, Green Yellow, Blue Black...

**Gelatos® and gel sticks**
Faber Castell make a product called 'Gelatos®' aimed at artists, and another identical one
called 'Gel Sticks', aimed at children. The only differences between the two are the price and the
range of colours available.
Gelatos/gel sticks are smooth and creamy acid-free pigment sticks.
They are very fun to use and glide easily on paper, canvas and wood.
The colours are vibrant and can be easily blended with your fingers, with or without water.
If you would like to experiment with them then just get one or two for now. If you want to start with
a good selection without the price tag, I recommend getting the set of 12 gel sticks + the Tropical
Gelatos® set of magenta, purple, lime green and turquoise (the colours I use most often).

## What about mediums?

**Gesso**
As a mixed media artist, gesso is necessity, not a luxury!
You will use it to prime your surface so it is ready to accept paint (especially if you work in an art
journal), to cover an element or layer you don't like, to provide an opaque base so your colours
stay true, to increase the opacity of your paint, and as a paint when a little white is required (it can
also be tinted with a little acrylic!)...
It comes in clear, white and black but white is the one you will need the most.
Get yourself a tub/jar and pour some into a small airtight plastic container that you can take it with
you if you travel or when you quickly need to get some with your fingers!

**Modelling paste** (also called molding paste)
Modelling paste is a white opaque paste that will allow you to create beautiful texture when applied with a palette/painting knife/plastic card. It can be used as is or mixed with your acrylic paints. Use it over a stencil for instant awesomeness or embed objects in it for a 3D piece!

**Gel medium**
Gel medium is a clear substance that looks a bit like hair gel. It is great for extending color, adhering collage pieces together and providing a 'clean' surface between layers.
For example, if you used water-soluble art supplies that 're-activate' (such as Gelatos/watercolours/Neocolour II crayons), and want to add more wet media on top, chances are, you will ruin what you just did as soon as you add water. To avoid 're-activation', add gel medium over your dry layer so you can safely paint over later it on. If you are unsure if or how things will react, I recommend adding gel medium between layers - better to be safe than sorry!

# Toys for artists!

In the mixed media world, what I consider a toy is any thing that allows me to create a little awesomeness without much effort: stencils, stamps, hand carved stamps, objects that create funky texture and marks...
Again, the available options are huge so, what to get first?

## Stamps
Stamps that will allow you to create background texture such as lines, dots, circles, geometric patterns and so on are great to start with as they are versatile. A stamp with an 'obvious' design can be great too but ask yourself first how often you will actually be using that design!
A stamp with Santa and 'ho ho ho' for example would probably be left alone for 11 months of the year so, not an ideal investment unless you specialise in Christmas art!
Stamps with reasonably abstract motifs are also great to have: I often use designs with flourishes, paisleys, spirals and flowers (just the head of the flower without stem or leaves) as they give subtle interest to my paintings (and create pretty texture at the same time).

## Stencils and Masks
Awww... So much fun to be had with those!
You can use them to preserve or cover parts of your painting, add modelling paste to create fantastic 3D texture in just a few seconds, stipple paint over or through to create interesting shapes and 3D texture.

Most popular sizes are 6x6 in and 12x12 in and, there are SO many designs to choose from!
But, which ones should you actually spend your precious money on? Well, just like stamps, I would only recommend starting with designs that you really love and that you can easily re-use over and over... That means anything with a reasonably abstract design or geometric pattern that will be suitable for most paintings you want to create.

I find that round/circular designs are the ones I use the most because I can use the whole stencil to create a focal point, or repeat the design many times to create a background. I also love the ones with smaller designs like leaves, geometric shapes and dots of various sizes (dots are excellent to add subtle pop in your paintings, either in the background or foreground).

# A few handy tips...

## Cleaning

I always keep a rag nearby to quickly wipe my dirty paint brushes and remove excess paint
(an old tea towel or towel cut in smaller pieces work just fine).
A roll of paper towels is also handy to have to remove excess water from a clean brush.

Baby wipes are a life-saver and a must-have in my studio! They are great to:
- Quickly remove paint and other yucky things from your hands, meaning you don't have to leave
  your painting in progress (I find that they actually work faster and better than soap and water!)
- Magically 'wipe' away a mistake before it dries on your surface (and sometimes your clothes
  so you may want to wear an apron or an old T-shirt!)
- Clean up your work surface while you are painting and when you are done
They are so cheap I promise you won't regret getting a pack!

## Drying your art

You and I are only human and I don't know anyone who wants to watch paint dry so...
To speed things up a little between layers, I like to use a travel size hair dryer.
I keep it on the edge of my studio table and always plugged in.
Because I use it often, I don't want to have to look for it whenever I need a quick blast of heat!
You can also use a heat tool specially made for crafting. With either one, remember to always stay
about 4 in (10 cm) above your surface and never for more than a few seconds in the same spot to
avoid potentially burning your paint or making it crack.
If you are lucky enough to have been given the Gift of Patience, please forget the above and let
things dry naturally :)
*Just keep in mind that acrylic paint dries quickly on the surface but may still be wet underneath,
especially when it has been applied as a thick layer.*

## How to protect your beautiful paintings

Once your final layer is thoroughly dry, you will want and need to protect your beautiful painting!
If you are working on canvas board, canvas or acrylic paper, I recommend a spray varnish instead
of a liquid one. It is much easier to apply and will give you more even results with no brush strokes.
Varnish comes in gloss, satin and matt - choose the finish you prefer.
I always go for gloss because it makes my colours just a little more vibrant than matt or satin.
Spray outside to avoid nasty smells! Do two coats both horizontally and vertically, letting each layer
dry between each coats.

If you are working in an art journal and find that your pages are sticking together, simply turn a
white wax candle (any kind or length) on its side and rub your pages with it in both directions and,
there you go: no more sticky pages and your art is protected!

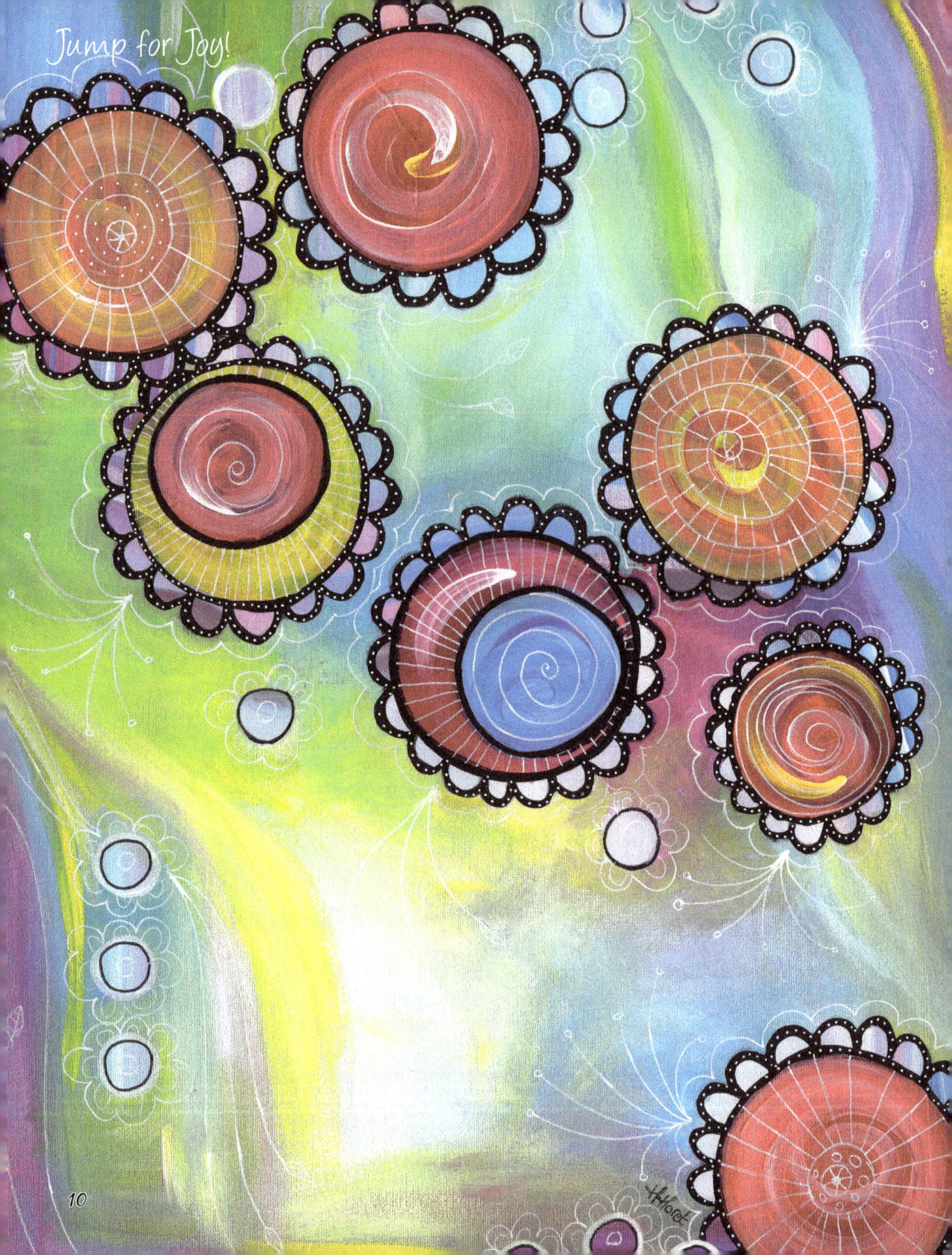
Jump for Joy!

# Essential supplies

## My recommended mixed media shopping list!

The supplies below are the ones I use all the time in my art, and the basic ones you will need to create the tutorials in this book. Please note I do not have any affiliation with any of the products mentioned in my book/website/videos, I simply recommend them because:
- *I have tested them and love to use them in my personal and professional work*
- *I know they are good quality and will last you a long time*
- *They are versatile enough to be re-used in your art, long after finishing this book*
- *They are stocked by most arts and craft stores*

You can of course substitute any of them with what you prefer/find, these are just my suggestions :)

**ESSENTIAL**
- **Brushes: square 3/4 in (2 cm) wash brush + fine tip brush**
- **Tools: old plastic credit/store card, small foam/latex make-up sponges**
- **Acrylic paint: magenta, dark purple, dark turquoise, lime green, yellow, orange, red, black, white**
- **White gesso**
- **Gel medium**
- **Gloss spray varnish (not needed if you only work in an art journal)**
- **Black Faber Castell Gelato or gel stick**
- **Markers: gold and black with large tip (2.5 mm) + black with fine tip (0.7 mm)**
- **Fine tip gel pen (white)**
- **Stencils: Tim Holtz 'Bubble' and 'Dot Fade', a large-ish round 'flower' stencil of your choice**
- **A couple of stamps of your choice**
- **Inkpad: Stazon 'Stone Gray'**
- **Disposable palette**

**OPTIONAL**
- **Tools:** small foam brush
- **Acrylic paint**: light pink, light turquoise, light purple/mauve, light green (or you can just add white to your essential colours to make lighter shades).
  If you can only get a handful of paint tubes then just get: white, black, red, yellow and blue then experiment with mixing your own colours (it's fun!)
- **Iridescent acrylic paint:** gold, Pébéo iridescent 'Blue Green' and 'Blue Red' but if you don't like the shiny effect then skip the tutorial steps where these paints are used
- **Washi tape:** Only used in one project so if you don't have any or don't want to buy any then simply follow the instructions in Chapter 4 to create your own.

If you are interested in finding out what my favourite tools, paints and mediums are, and where to buy them, visit this page on my website:

mimibondi.com/my-favourite-art-supplies

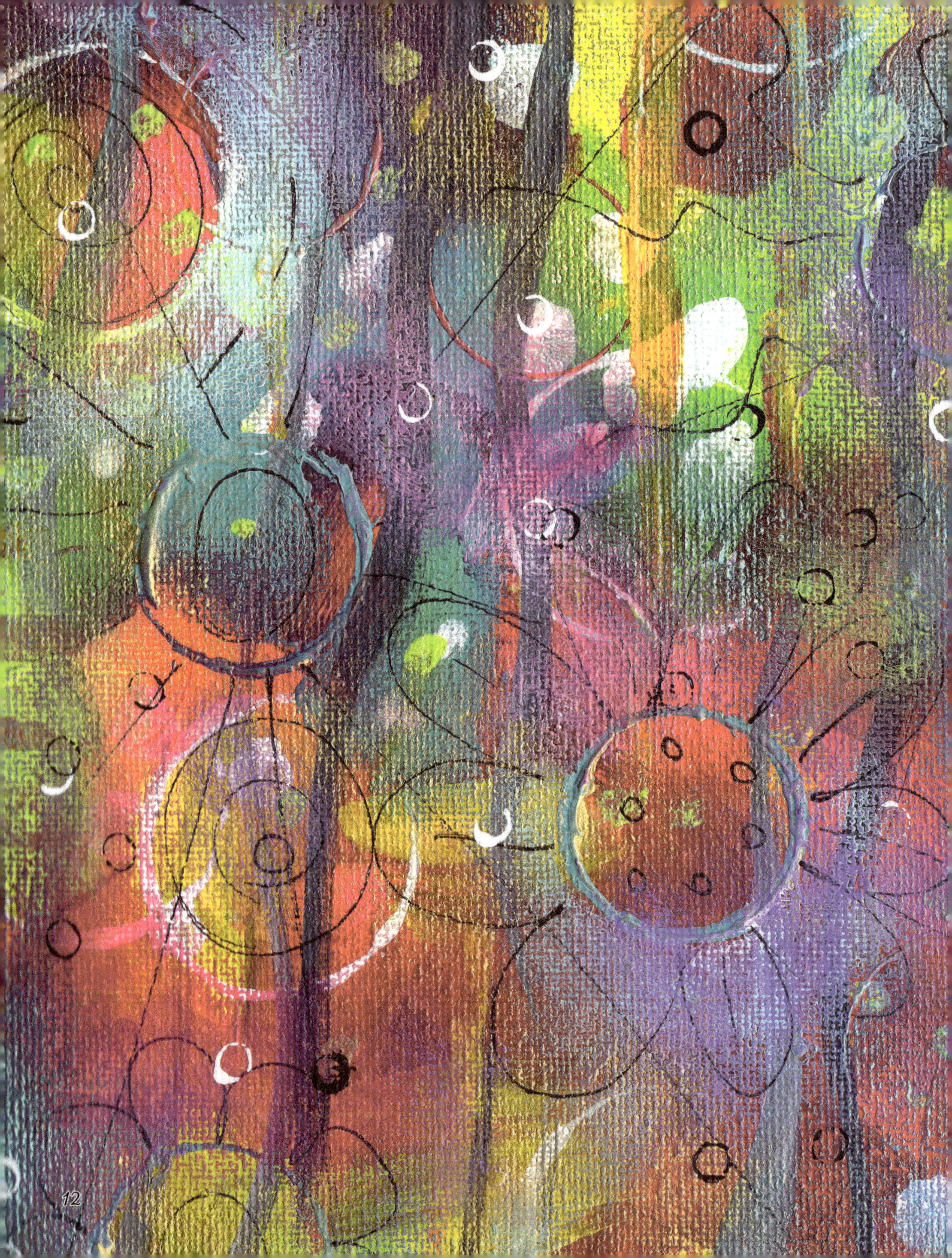

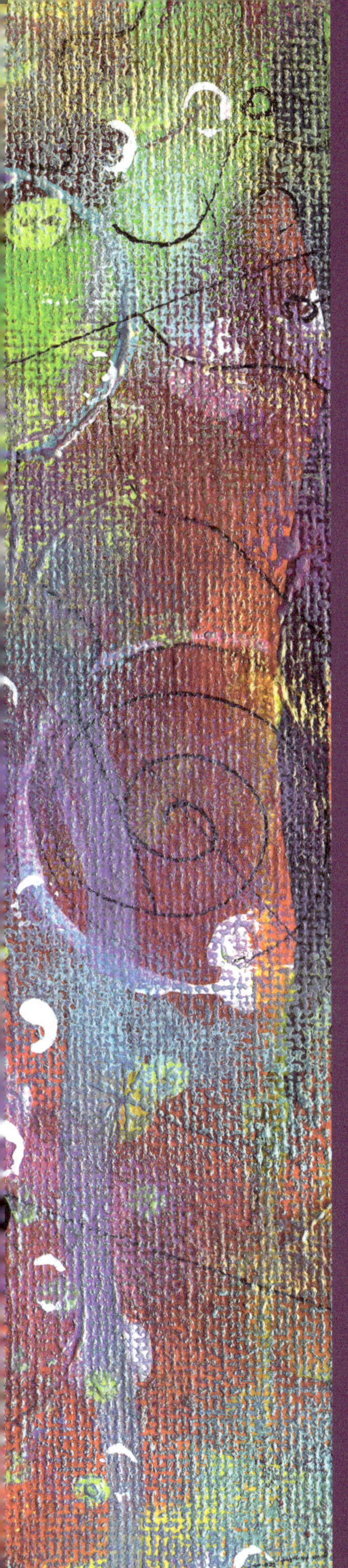
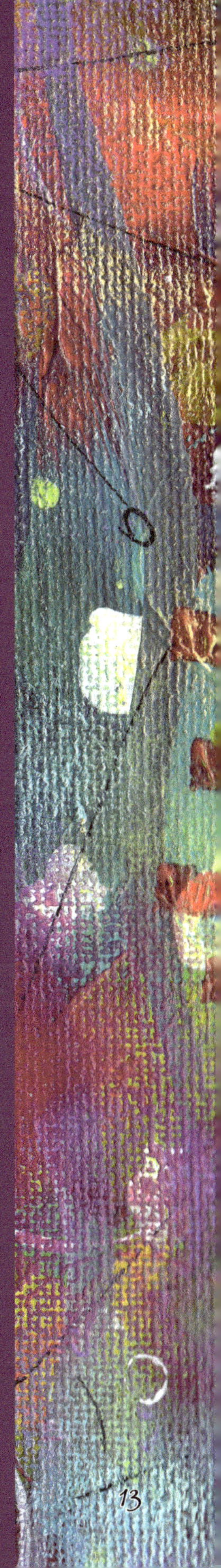

# Loosen up
# and Let go

## Are you ready?

This first chapter will help you release any fear that may be blocking you from getting into creating art!

I will show you the technique I use to start most of my paintings, the one that allows me to 'warm up' and get the juices flowing! It is such a great way to relax and forget the madness of life (at least for a little while)...

At the end of this project, you will realise how easy and fun painting can be and will have gained some new (or renewed) confidence so... Don't stop there, keep going!

Just remember to focus on the journey more than the destination and that, if things don't turn out how you wanted them to, you can easily paint over and start again.

Ready? Put your favourite music on, relax your shoulders and let's have fun with paint!

## Recommended supplies

• Acrylic paint: magenta, yellow, red, white, light green, turquoise
• Black fine tip marker

Optional:
• Gold acrylic paint
• Pébéo Iridescent acrylic paint 'Blue Green'

# I'm here with you, every step of the way!

**1** My favourite brush is a 3/4 in (2 cm) square brush with synthetic bristles because it is great for spreading paint around quickly and blending colours together. On the photo, both have Taklon bristles but the left brush has a wooden handle and the right one, a plastic handle. I love and use both but as mentioned earlier, I recommend plastic as it will last you longer than wood. Of course, you could also just use your fingers for the following steps!

**2** Let's start by squeezing a few blobs of paint on your palette: magenta, red, turquoise and yellow. I chose these colours because they are contrasting and vibrant, and won't create muddy colours when mixed together. Feel free to choose less colours, or different ones!

**3** Now is the time to switch off your brain and block out any negative thoughts popping up... Your only goal in life right now is to cover your surface in random patches of colour! So dip your slightly damp brush in yellow and... Go nuts!! Create a rough yellow patch by moving your brush left to right and up and down until you have almost no paint left on your brush (don't press to hard). Repeat in a few areas on your surface and don't stress about making perfect little patches, we just want them to be rough, nothing fancy!

**4** Now pick up some magenta (no need to rinse your brush as a nice orange will be created from blending magenta and yellow), and spread it like you did before...

**5** Rinse your brush, pick up some turquoise and continue the process. Feel free to overlap and blend some of the various colours together: turquoise and yellow will give you a lovely green, turquoise and magenta will create a nice purple so, no fear!

Cover most of your surface with those three colours. Don't worry if you can see a little bit of your surface below as we will be covering most of it later on. This is just our first layer.

**6** Clean your brush, pick up some red and dab your brush on your surface, blending some of the colours together in some areas, and simply making red 'squares' in others. You want to create a little variation so not everything needs to be nicely blended. If you 'over-blended', it's OK! Leave your painting to dry then just add a few more patches of red. It's that easy :-)

**7** Remember to always dry each layer before moving on to the next... You can of course let your painting air dry but, if you're impatient like me (blowing on it does not work so save your breath!), then grab a heat tool or hair dryer. Just take care not to stay in the same area for more than a few of seconds at a time to avoid potentially burning the top layer of paint.

# Release the child in you!

**8** When everything is completely dry, dip your finger in yellow paint and let's get ready for some childish fun...!

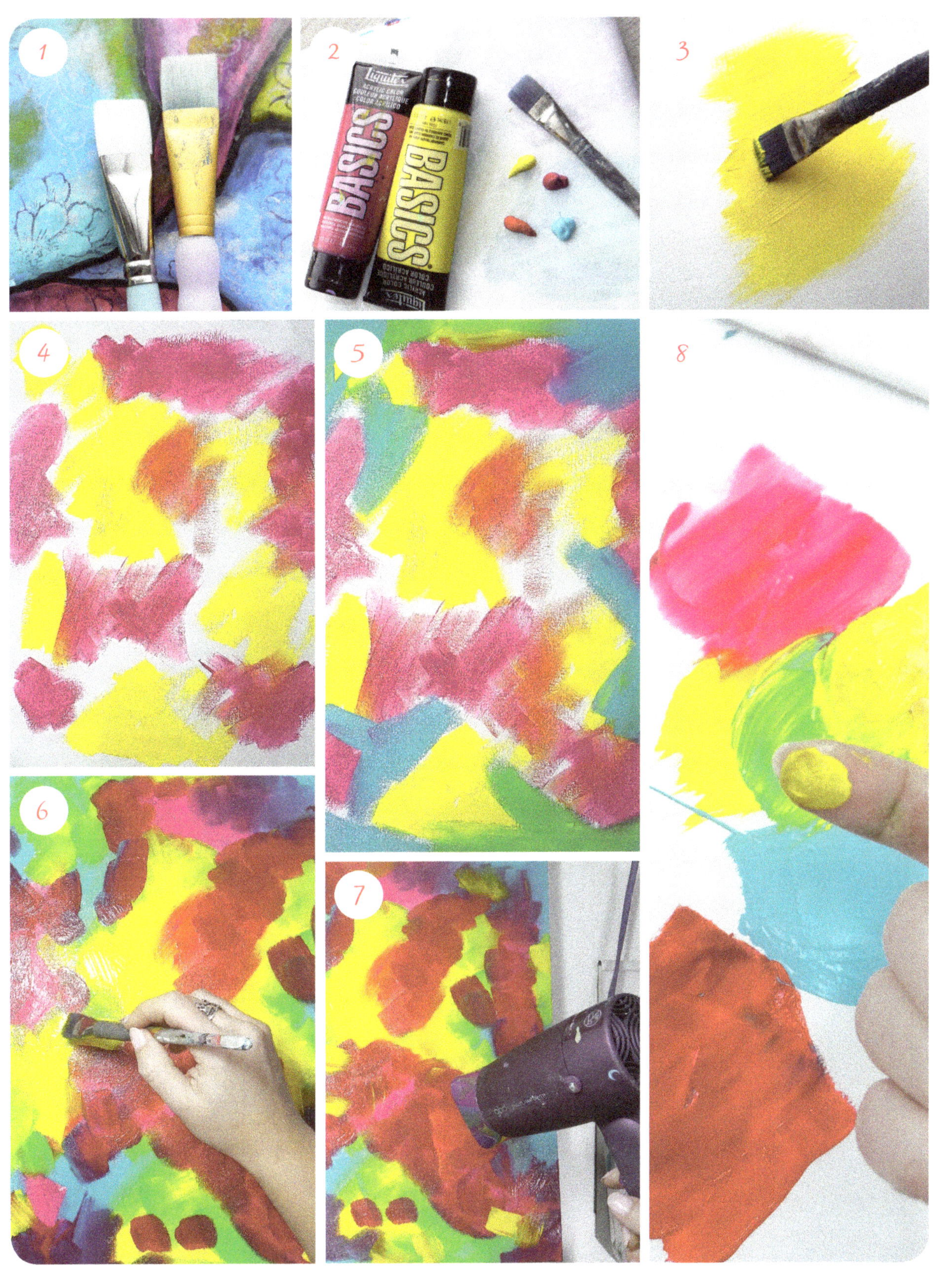

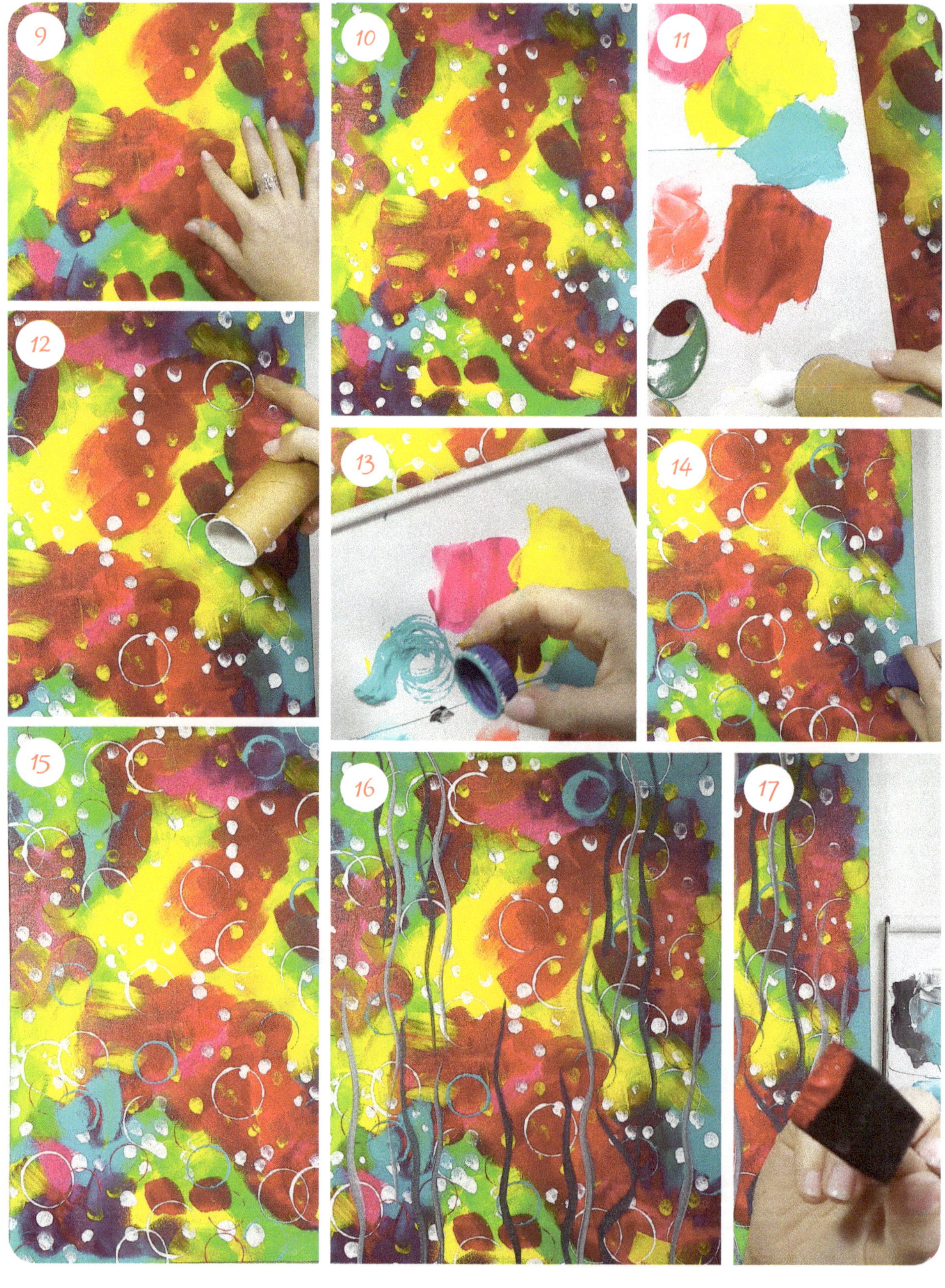

**9** Randomly dab your finger all over your surface to create little dots, varying the pressure to get different sizes... Just have fun with it, there is no wrong way to do this!

**10** Move on to white paint and repeat the process...

**11** Now find a toilet paper roll (or similar object) and dip the rim in a large blob of white paint. You could dip your finger in the paint and rub it onto the rim if you prefer.

**12** Press the rim down on your surface to create circles. They don't need to be perfect! In fact, it's more interesting if they are uneven, like this one here...

**13** Find another round object with a smaller diameter (here I am using the cap of a plastic bottle) to create more circles, this time with turquoise paint.

**14** Press the cap in areas where you don't have white circles but also overlap a few of them to create more interest.

**15** Find an even smaller round object (such as a smaller bottle cap or paint tube cap) and create a few more circles with magenta paint (these will be more subtle). This is fun, right? Can you resist the temptation to cover the entire surface with circles? I have to hold back!

## Let's create a few more interesting marks...

**16** Mix a little black with white on your palette to create a dark grey. Dip your square brush in the paint and create wavy lines coming up from the bottom edge of your surface.

Repeat with lines coming from the top edge then add a little more white to your dark grey to get a lighter shade. Paint a few more lines between the dark grey ones, varying the pressure as you go.

**17** If you have a small foam brush, dip it in red paint.
If you don't, simply use your square brush, a fine tip brush or your finger... Improvise!
Your marks don't have to be exactly the same as mine to create a great painting...

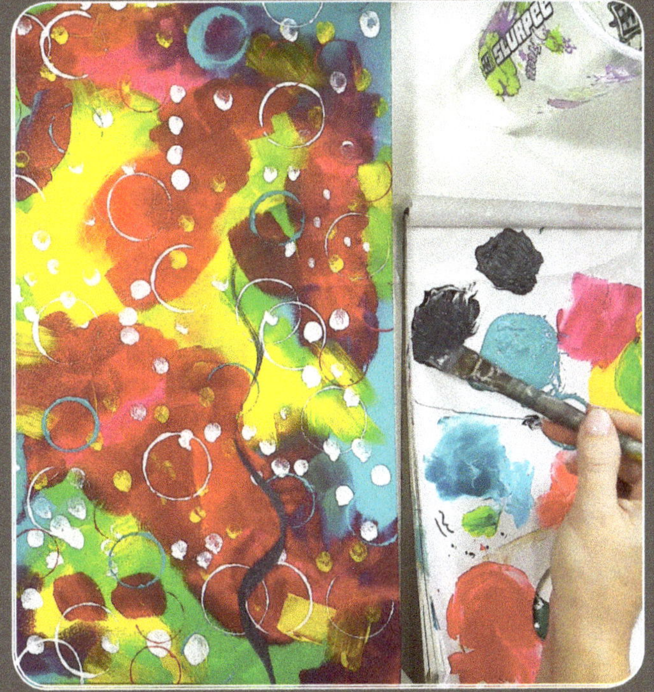

18  Dab your foam brush on one of the edges of your surface to create fat irregular lines.
Again, feel free to experiment with pressure and keep things uneven! Paint a cluster of
marks (it doesn't matter how many) on one edge and repeat on the other three edges.

19  Dip your foam brush in yellow paint (no need to clean it first) and create a few more marks.
See how you can get an interesting 'spotted' effect without even trying?

20  Dip your foam brush in more yellow and add a few wavy lines...
Some coming from the edges of your surface...

21  ... And some from the middle of your surface.
Feel free to vary the thicknesses and length of your lines for more interest.

22  Now grab a fine tip brush, dip it in light green paint and dab it on your surface to create
little dots throughout (they will be more visible on top of darker colours like red and
magenta here for example). You can create little clusters of dots, place them on lines
or spirals... You could even 'write' something personal or meaningful in dots as this will
be covered later on - just have fun with it and remember: no thinking allowed!

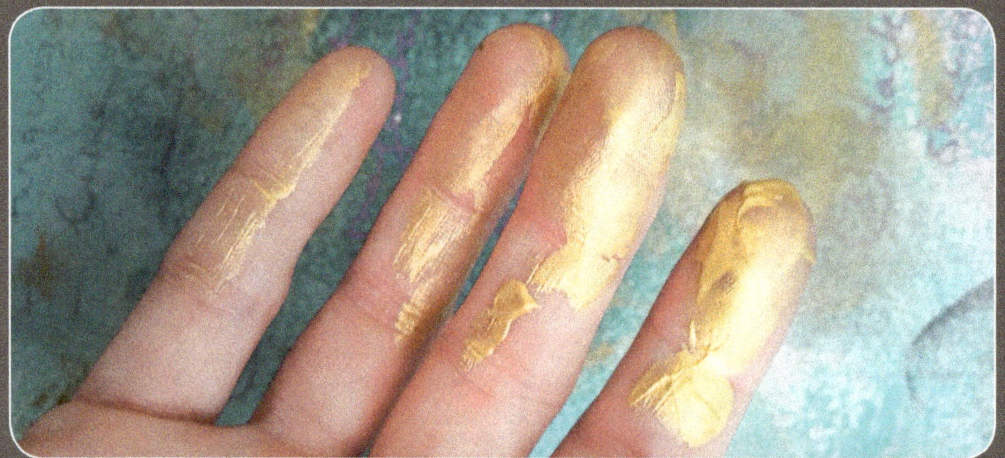

## Now let's get our fingers dirty!!

23  If you like shiny things as much as I do, then you will enjoy this step! Squeeze a pea-size dot
of gold paint onto your fingertip and spread the paint on your surface in a few areas:
imagine you are 'massaging' your canvas/paper by moving your hand in a circular
motion and spreading it outwards until you have not paint left on your finger(s).

24  Here you can see the reflection of a few patches of gold paint. The paint stays a little
transparent when applied in thin layers - feel free to add as little or as much as you like!

25  Let dry then add a little white paint to the turquoise on your palette, dip your finger(s) in it
and rub the paint unevenly around some of the white circles created earlier.

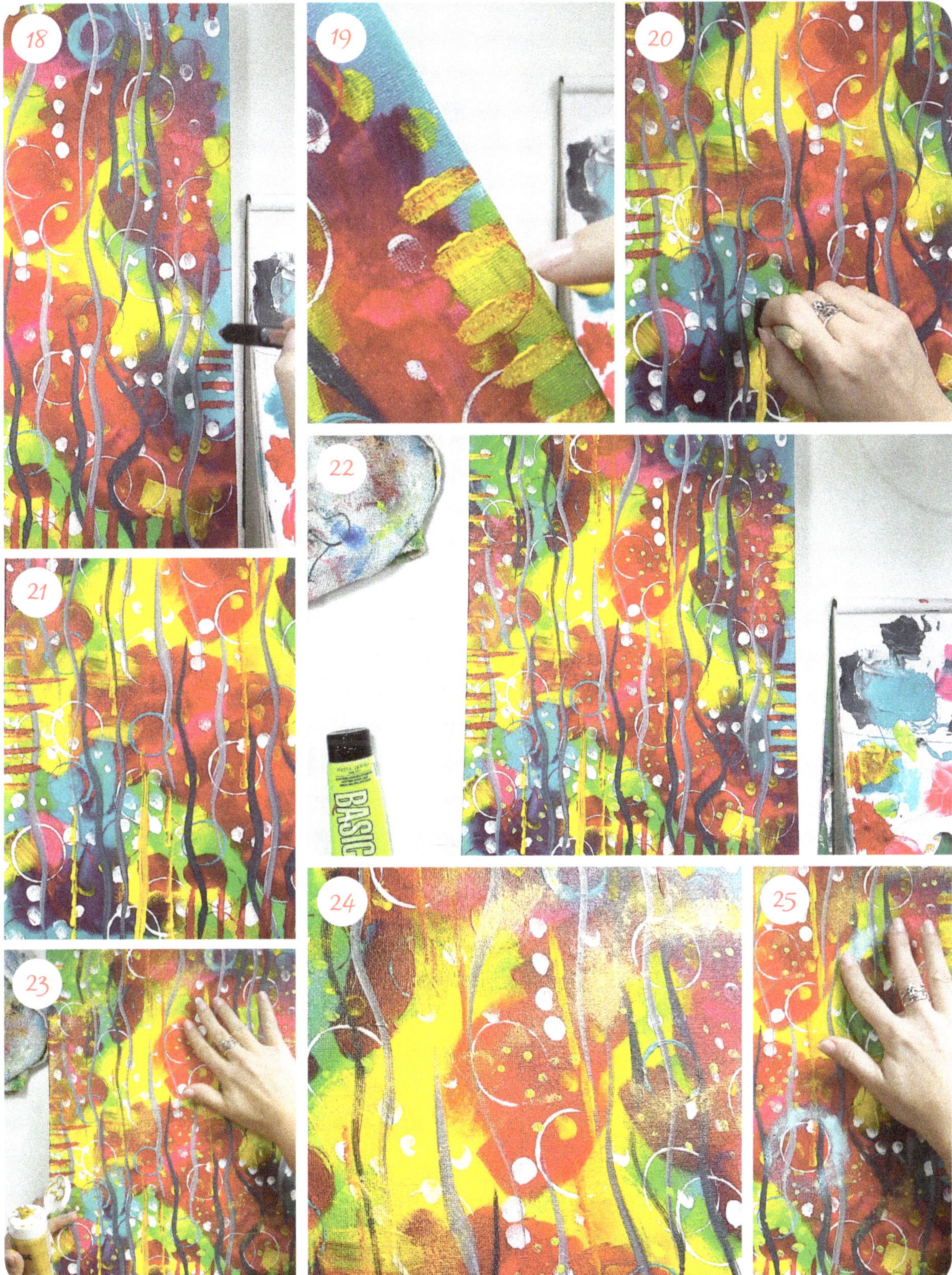

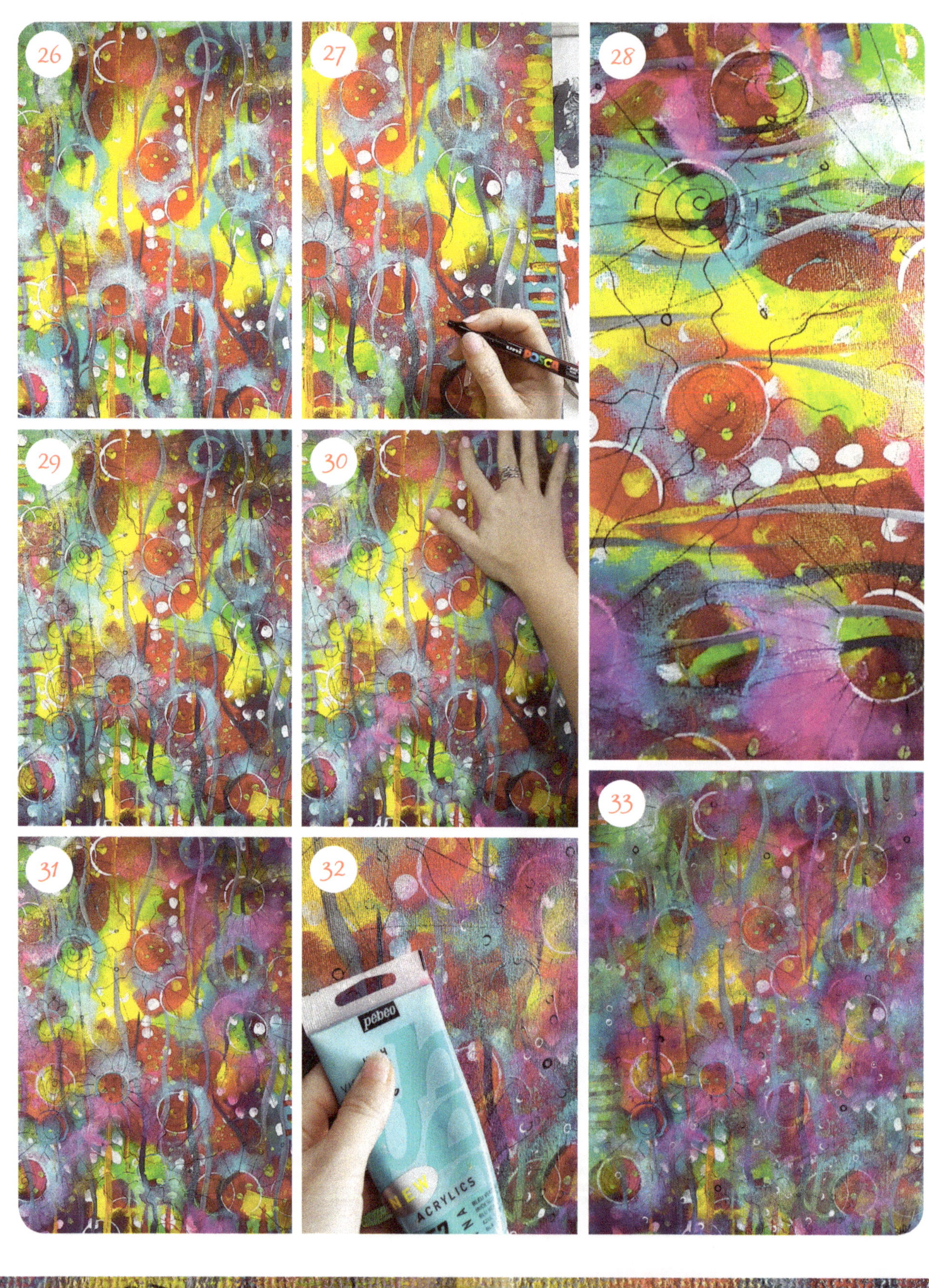

**26** Next, rub a little 'pure' turquoise around some of the circles and partly over the edges of your surface... Experiment with varying the pressure of your finger(s): a light touch and a little paint will allow the background to show through while a thick layer or firm pressure will create opacity (useful to block out anything you may not like in the background).
There is no right or wrong way to do this! Again, just have fun with it and don't worry about the end result because whatever you do, it will look awesome in the end, I promise!

## It's doodle time!

**27** Time to get a little more creative with some funky doodles...
Make sure everything is thoroughly dry as any slightly damp area will ruin your pen!
Here I am using a 0.7 mm tip black Posca paint pen but anything similar will work (you could also use a fine tip brush and diluted black paint, or black ink).

**28** If you have never doodled before, well, there isn't much to it! Here are a few simple ideas:
- Pick one of the circles on your surface and draw some long loose 'petals' around it
- Choose another circle and draw some fat 'petals' this time
- Draw some wavy lines around another circle
- Try some spirals in the middle of some of the circles (big and small)
- Add small black circles in between the larger circles
- Draw some dashed lines, dotted lines... Anything that comes to mind!

**29** This should be fun and relaxing, don't over think it! Just let your hand decide where to go...

**30** Back to paint! Add a little magenta on your finger and, just like you did with turquoise earlier, rub the paint around some of the circles (you can go over the turquoise) and also in other areas if you wish (you don't have to stick to circles only!).

**31** Mix a little turquoise and magenta on your palette to create some purple and rub a little here and there. Let everything dry and repeat with a little yellow or light green.

**32** Optional: Add blue iridescent paint on your finger and spread it on some of the dry areas and also where the paint is still a bit wet so it blends with the colours you just added.

**33** And... Just like that, you finished your first painting! Stand back and admire what you just accomplished: look at the various layers you created, how some elements show through clearly while others are a little hidden and create mystery, how the metallic shine reflect in the light, how the colours pop in some areas but are more subtle in others...
Note: if there is anything you are not that happy with then it's easy to adjust:
- You can disguise a doodle by rubbing some paint over it
- Emphasize a colour by rubbing a little more of that colour on top or
- If you find that a colour you liked in the earlier layers is not really obvious anymore
  then add some more on the top. It really is up to you!
You can proudly hang your painting on your wall after varnishing it or, if you are feeling more adventurous, use it as a background to create something even more awesome!

*The finished painting is showcased on page 102*

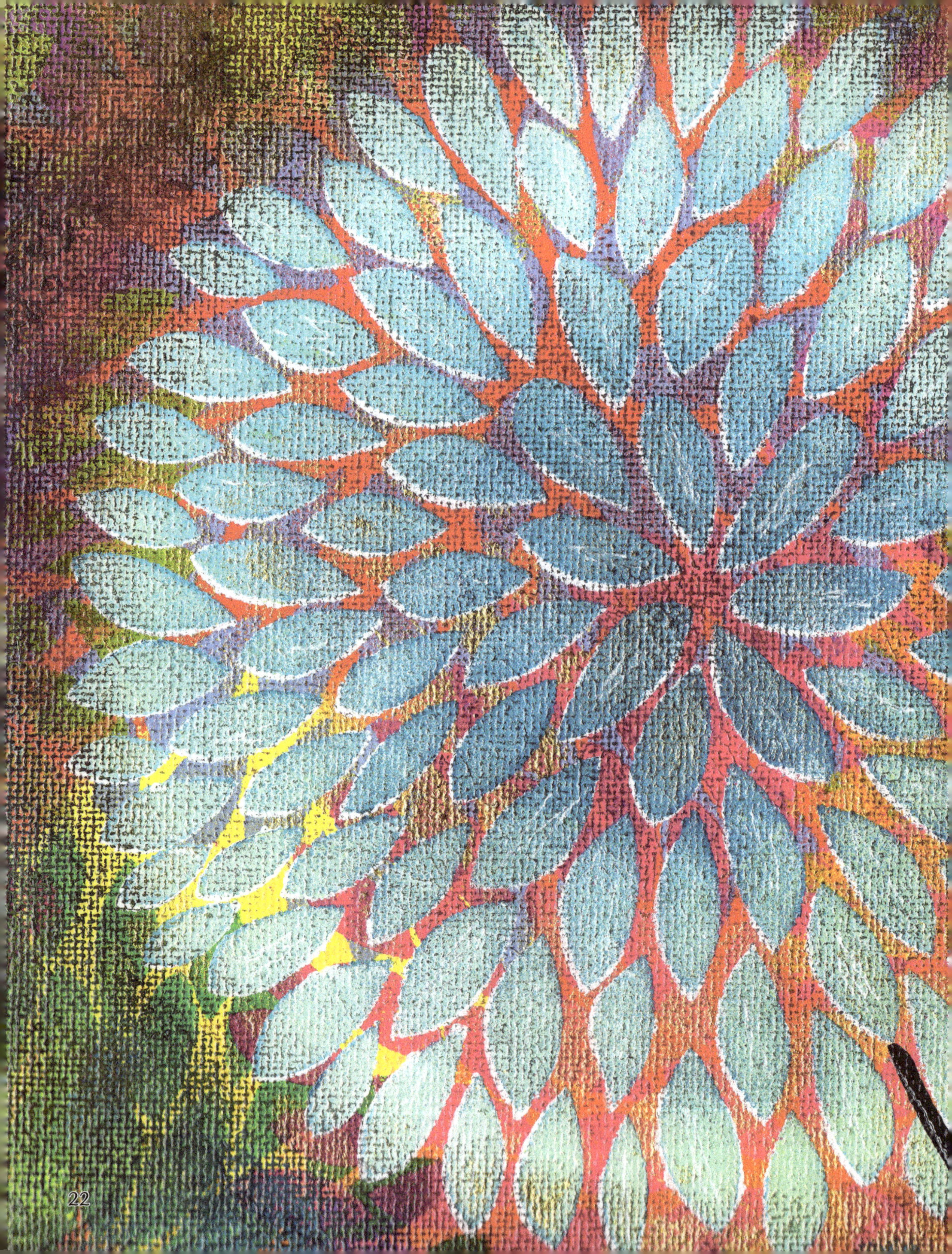

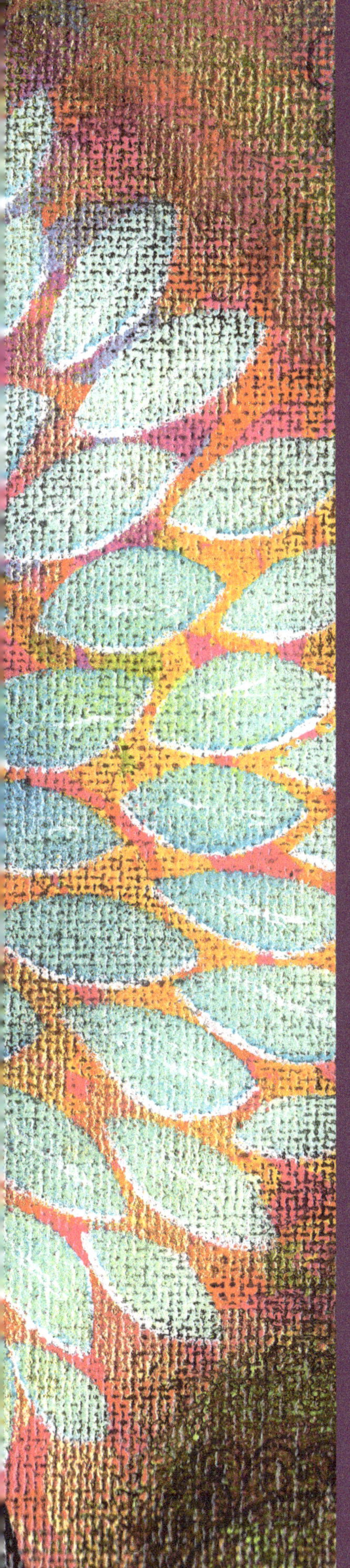
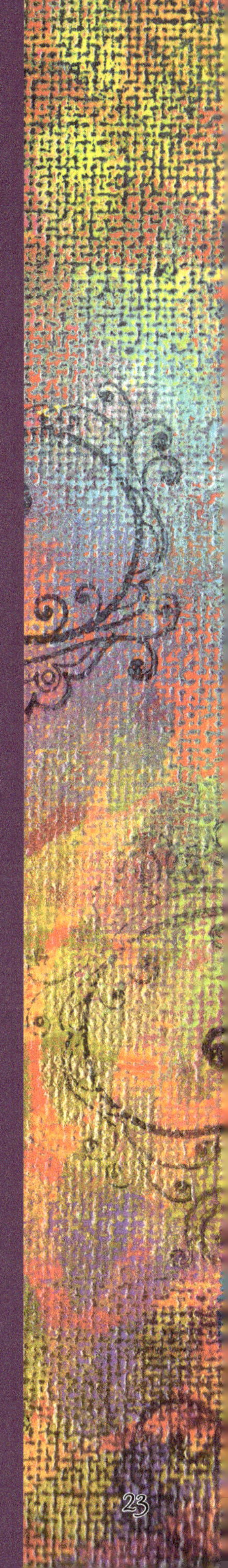



# Grow
## and Bloom

## One stencil for all!

Who said creating layers was difficult? Nonsense! In this project, I will show you how to create a beautiful background with a lot of texture and depth using just one stencil and some paint!

You will then use the same stencil to create a focal point, and learn how to add depth and shadows to make it really pop.

When you are done with this project, I want you to apply the techniques you just learnt: start a new painting using different colours and a different stencil for a completely different result!

Once you see what amazing art you can create with very few supplies, I know you will get excited by the possibilities!
I am excited for you too ;-)

## Recommended supplies

- Acrylic paint: yellow, magenta, red, pink, lime green, light blue, light purple, green, deep turquoise, black, white
- White gesso
- Round stencil that evokes the shape of a flower (but it doesn't have to be one!)
- Black Gelato/gel stick
- Stamp of your choice (nothing chunky)
- 'Stone Gray' Stazon inkpad
- Fine tip white gel pen

## A sunny start...

**1** Using your slightly damp square brush, pick up a little yellow paint and spread it onto your surface in various directions. Create a few yellow patches around your surface.

**2** Repeat with magenta then red, spreading the paint without thinking too much and with no particular aim other than covering the whole surface ('patchy' is perfectly OK)!

**3** You can overlap the colours, blend some of them together, spread the paint with your fingers... There are no rules here so have fun with it! No need to make it perfect as we will be covering most of it later on... Let everything dry.

## Stencil magic!

**4** Select a round stencil (any design that is not overly detailed will work well), ideally about 1/4 or so of your surface in diameter (my stencil is 6x6 in). You will also need makeup sponges or a kitchen sponge cut into little squares (a cheap, dense one with no texture works best). You can use a small sponge for each colour we are going to use, or just one you will need to wash and dry between each layer.

**5** Pick three paint colours that contrast well with your first layer (light blue, mauve and lime green for example) and squeeze out a pea-size blob of each on your palette (you won't need much and you can always add more later if needed).

**6** Dab a sponge in mauve paint then tap it in a dry area of your palette to remove excess paint. You just want a thin layer of paint on the sponge to avoid seepage under the stencil.

**7** Place your stencil in the top left corner of your surface and hold it firmly with one hand. If you prefer, you can use masking tape (or washi tape) to hold it in place. Dab your sponge over the stencil in an 'up and down' motion, never from side to side to avoid paint going under the stencil. Don't panic if it does as it probably won't be visible later!

**8** Continue dabbing until the whole surface of the stencil is covered... One layer of paint will let you see what is underneath but if you would prefer the colours to be more opaque then it's best to apply two thin layers of paint rather than a thick one!

## On and on...

**9** Carefully remove the stencil and out loud, say: 'That looks awesome!' or any variant such as 'cool bananas!!' or 'blimey, I'm good!'. If there is any paint on the front or back of the stencil, use a dry rag/paper towel to remove it and... Let's do it again, shall we?? Repeat the process with lime green paint on the right side of your surface then blue at the bottom. Place the stencil over the edge to create more interest!

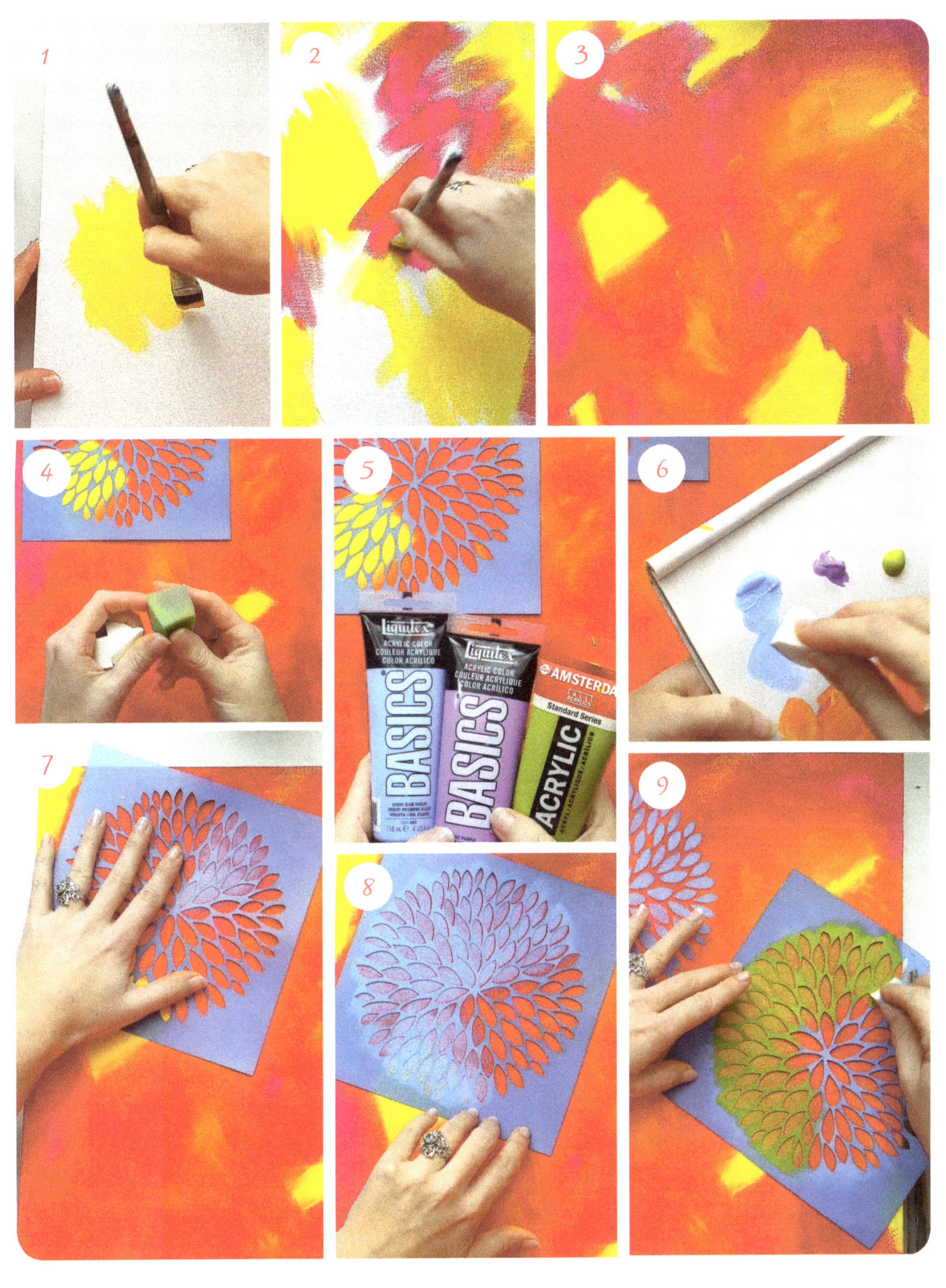

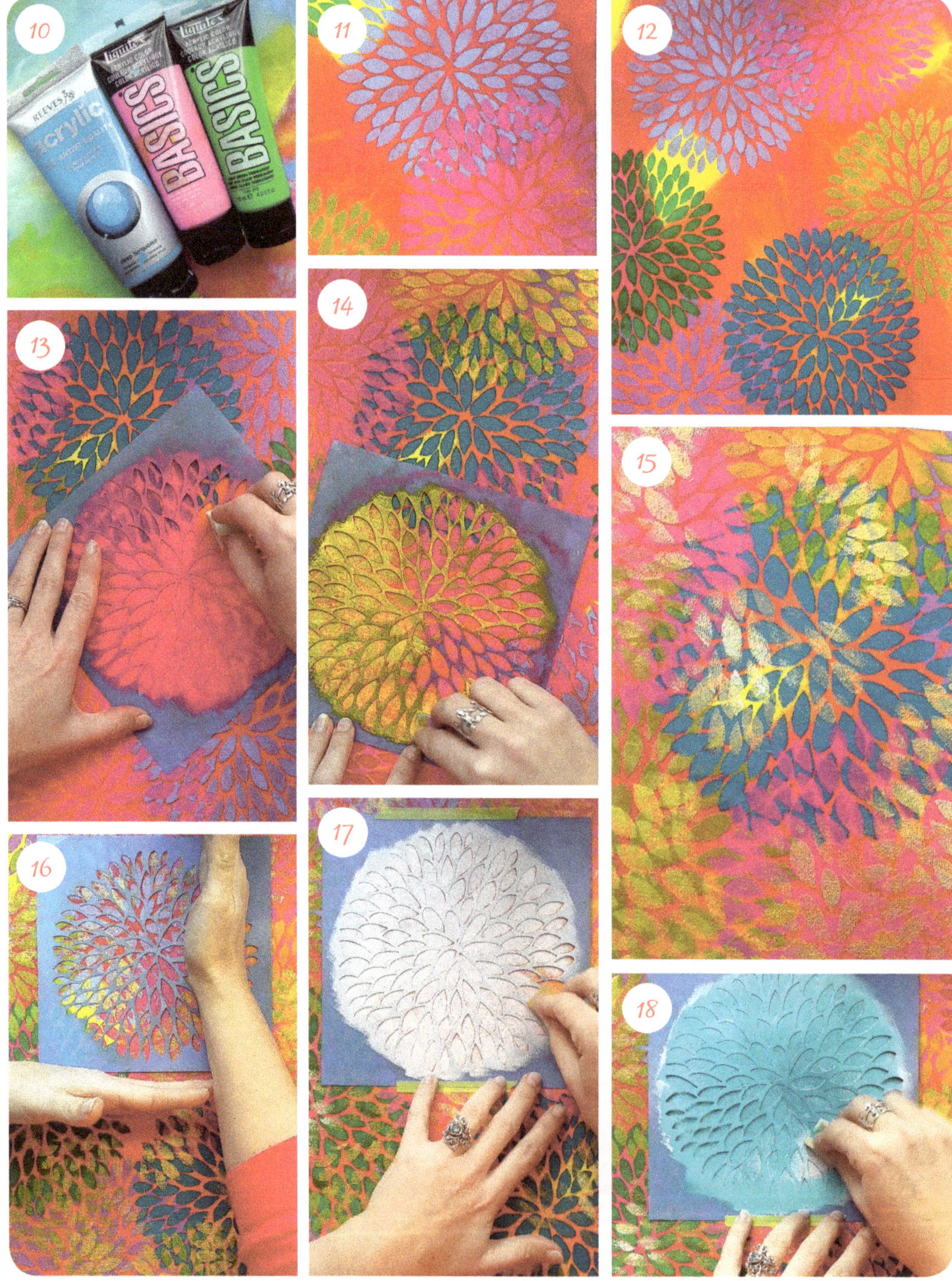

# New layers and new colours

**10** Pick three new colours, such as vibrant green, pink and deep turquoise.

**11** Place your stencil in a way that it overlaps at least one of the previous stencilled shapes or an edge of your surface, or both... Create a pink flower.

**12** Repeat with green, then turquoise.
You are slowly creating layers to give depth to your painting...

**13** Let everything dry, clean your stencil and sponge(s) if needed then add another pink flower. away from the first one. By now your surface should be mostly covered with flowers!

**14** If you find that your background has too much of one colour or doesn't 'pop' enough, add a couple of yellow flowers using the same yellow from your background). Let dry...

**15** Finally, dip your sponge into a little yellow and white (without mixing) and dab it over part of your stencil. Repeat here and there, over the other layers, to create extra interest and depth. Let everything dry thoroughly.

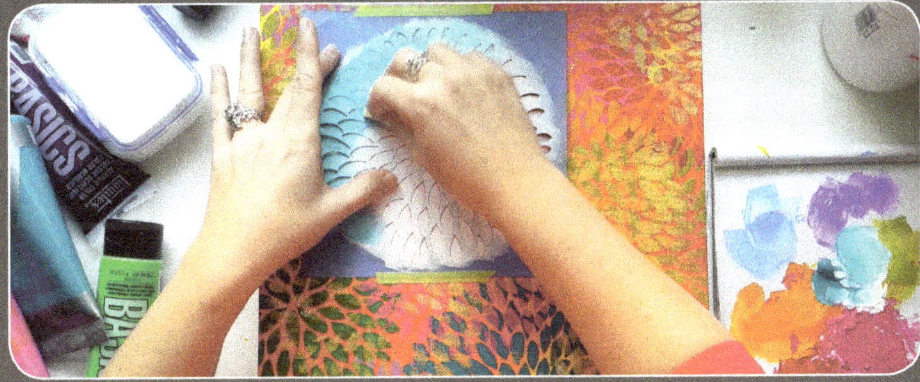

# Now let's create the star of the show!

**16** If you are unsure where to place your focal point, here is what I do: I visualise two lines dividing my surface into four equal sections - one going in the middle vertically and one in the middle horizontally. I place my stencil where the lines cross, then move it a little to the left and towards the top to get a visually well-balanced composition.

**17** For the following steps I suggest using masking tape or washi tape to hold your stencil down as we are going to create a few layers in the same area. We are now using gesso instead of paint to create an opaque base so that the colours of our main flower will really stand out from the background. Cover the whole stencil with a thin layer of gesso, let dry. Add another layer and let dry.

**18** Mix a little white paint to the turquoise you used before and stencil over the gesso.

**19** While the turquoise paint is still wet...
Add a little yellow to your turquoise/white mix on your palette to create a light green.
Dab your sponge on the outside edge of the stencil, then dab towards the center so
the light green 'fades' into the turquoise.

**20** While the paint is still wet, dab a clean sponge into white paint and lightly dab from the
outside edge of the stencil (the tips of the flower), slightly into the light green (remember to
always do this in an 'up and down' motion). This will create subtle shadows and highlights!

**21** Let dry and carefully remove the stencil. Stand back to admire your gorgeous flower!
You are allowed to tell the world how cool it looks.

**22** Dip your fine tip brush in black paint (add a little water to make it more fluid or use ink) and
draw a stem from the flower all the way to the bottom edge of your surface. Let dry.

## Finger painting time!

**23** For this step, try to leave a little unpainted gap (about 0.5 cm or 1/8 in) around the flower
and stem so you can still see the layers underneath.

Add a little light green paint on your fingertip then rub it in a circular motion near the flower
and stem, not right against it.

Switch to a little yellow, varying the pressure so parts of your layers underneath show more
than others. Repeat the process in turn with the colours you used on your background
flowers (pink, magenta, turquoise... Always with a little paint at a time). If you want your
colours to pop more, you can mix them with a little white to make them more opaque
(this will also make the colours a little lighter).

**24** Once you have added colourful little patches all around your flower and stem, add some
to your background here and there (don't cover everything!).
Let everything dry before moving on...

## Adding subtle details and texture...

**25** For this step, choose a stamp that has fairly fine details. Anything with swirls, spirals, curves
or even flowers will work. It doesn't really matter what you use as long as you get a little
contrast without distracting from the main focal point... If you are using a canvas like I am,
put a book underneath so you have a hard surface to stamp onto.
Stick your stamp on an acrylic block, press the inkpad over it and stamp your surface.

**26** Repeat the stamping process in various areas (around the flower and stem) making sure
the overall look is natural (that means nothing too symmetrical!). I was lucky to find a stamp
sheet set with various shapes in a similar design (it's called 'Artistic Flourish' by Inkadinkado).

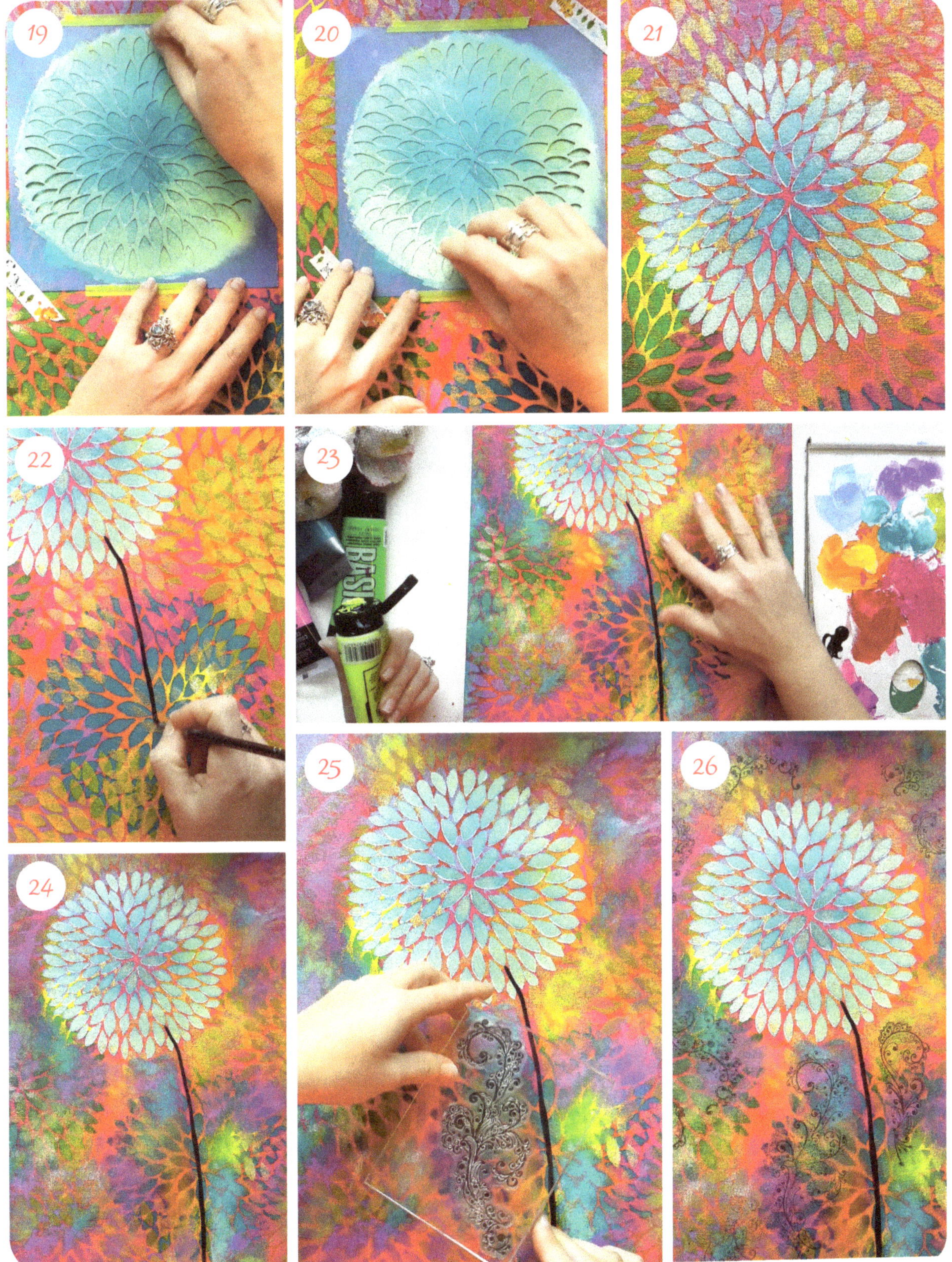

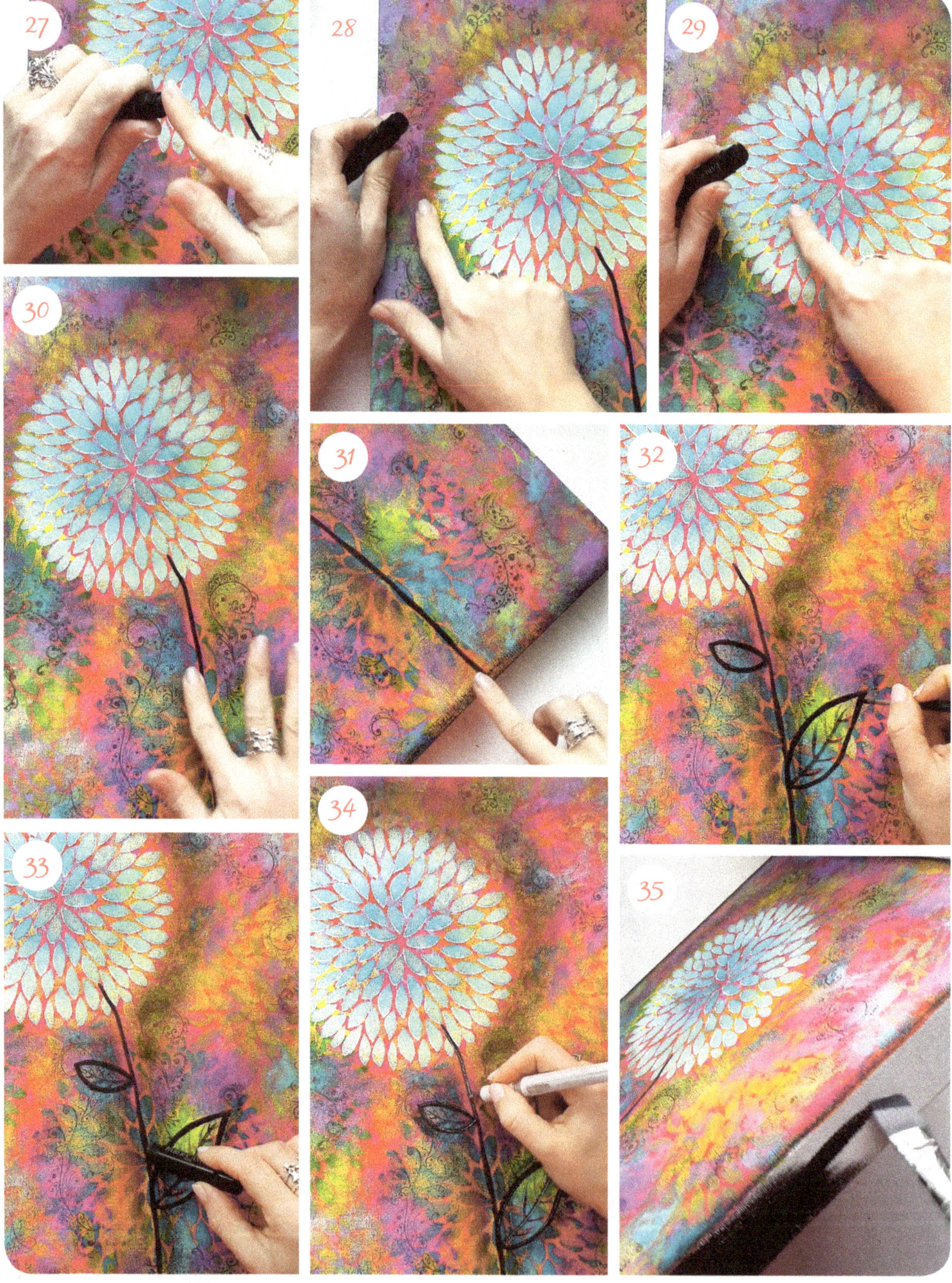

## Now let's create subtle shadows...

**27** My favourite tool for creating discreet shadows is a black Gelato/gel stick. Try it out!
Simply rub it directly onto your finger (don't worry, it washes off easily!)...

**28** ... Then rub your finger on your surface, where you want to create a shadow.
Add more on your finger when needed and keep going until the shadow is as dark or as light
as you want. Repeat all around the flower, keeping a slight gap so the background is visible.

**29** Add a little in the center around the dark turquoise petals to create a little depth...

**30** ... And also around the stem, keeping a little gap on both sides.

## Showcase your flower with a border and details

**31** Next, lightly rub the gelato stick straight onto the edges of your surface then your finger back
and forth over it to create a border. Add a little water on your finger to help with blending  if
you wish. Turn your surface around and repeat on the next edge until all sides are done.

**32** Dip your fine tip brush in black paint (or ink) and paint a couple of simple
leaves. Add some veins in the center of each one. Let dry.

**33** Rub the gelato stick around the leaves and blend with your finger, like you did earlier.

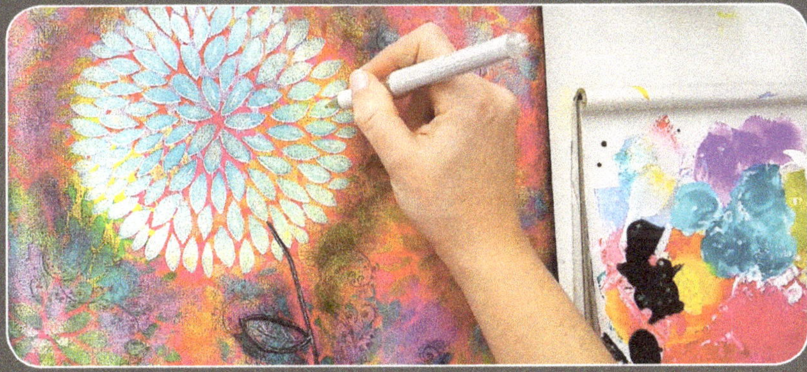

**34** Add fine details with a white gel pen (or white paint and extra fine tip brush): a line along
the middle of the stem, leaves and veins, and a few lines over the tips of the main flower.
Uneven lines are fine!

**35** If you are using a canvas, paint the edges with two coats of black (let dry between each
layer) to make your colours pop and echo the black used on the border, stem, leaves and
stamped details - but you could use other colours of course!
A couple of coats of varnish and you are ready to hang your new painting on the wall!

*The finished painting is showcased on page 105*

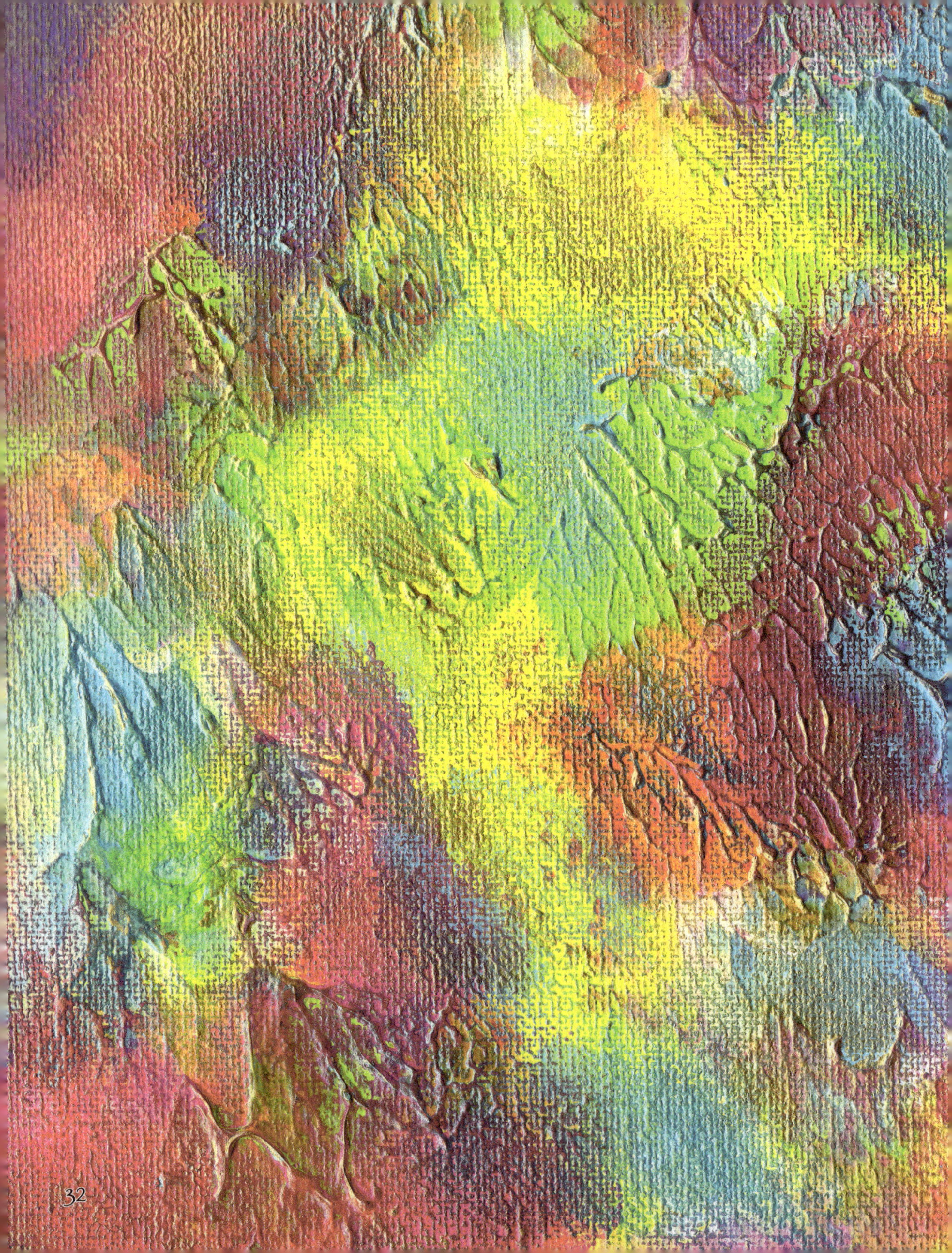

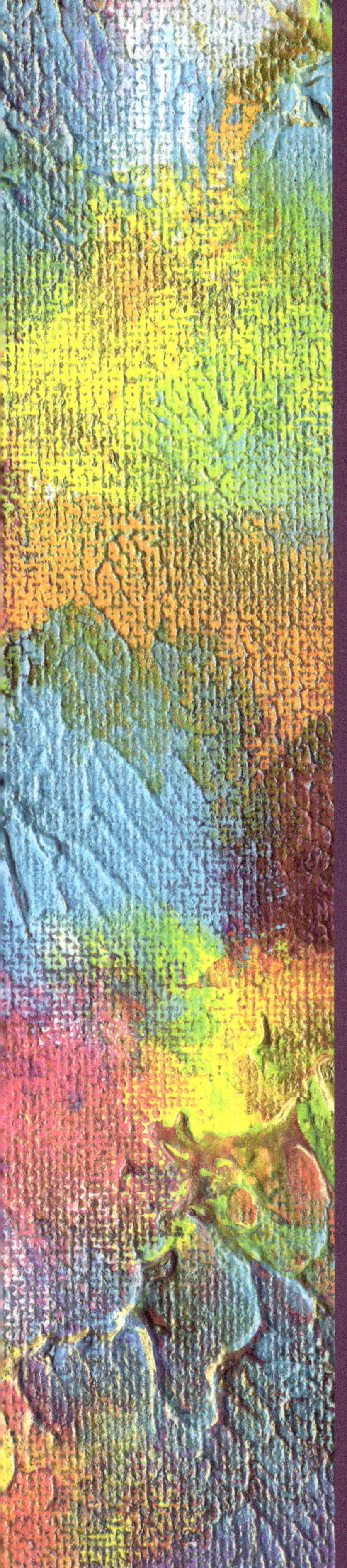

# 3

# Lost
## in a Dream

## 3D texture with paint

This is the easiest and most fun technique I know to get an amazing raised texture on a painting... Let me show you how to create it without any tools or mediums: all you need is a sheet of paper, some paint and your trusty hands!

You are going to love seeing this beautiful abstract piece full of detail, colour and shine develop in front of you!

What I enjoy so much about this style of abstract art is that, because there is no primary focal point, you can truly let your mind wander, using your imagination to interpret what is front of you.

Simply stop and study the texture, admire how the light reflects and how the colours draw you in... Let yourself relax... Ahhh....

Hang on, first we need to actually create this gorgeous dreamy painting!

## Recommended supplies

- Acrylic paint: light turquoise, light blue or mauve, pink, green, magenta, orange, yellow, light purple, white
- A sheet of acrylic paper the same size as your surface

Optional:
- Gold acrylic paint
- Pébéo Iridescent acrylic paint: 'Blue Green' and 'Red Blue'

# Creating texture is child's play!

1. Let's get started with the fun!
No matter what surface you are working on, just use a piece of paper about the same size as your surface. I am working on a 30x40cm canvas here and will use a sheet of acrylic paper about the same size. Thin cardstock or heavy paper will work too do but if you use acrylic paper, you can start a second painting at the same time with no paint wasted!

2. Choose three complementary colours for the first layer. Here I am using light turquoise, light mauve/blue and lime green but you could go a different road altogether and go with a combination of red, yellow and orange for example!

3. Squeeze out little blobs of light turquoise on your surface, straight from the tube, spacing them out randomly.

4. Without delay, repeat with lime green and light mauve/blue, then white.
Don't worry if you accidentally put a large blob! Just spread it out a little with your finger. It is not an exact science so just enjoy the process!

5. While the paint is still wet, grab your sheet of paper and gently cover your surface with it. Hold the center with one hand and smooth out the page in all directions with the other.

6. Hold and press the paper gently so you can feel the paint 'squish' a little underneath. The paint has been sandwiched so it's not going anywhere (although some may ooze out from the side if you added a blob close to the edge - that's OK, just wipe it off!).

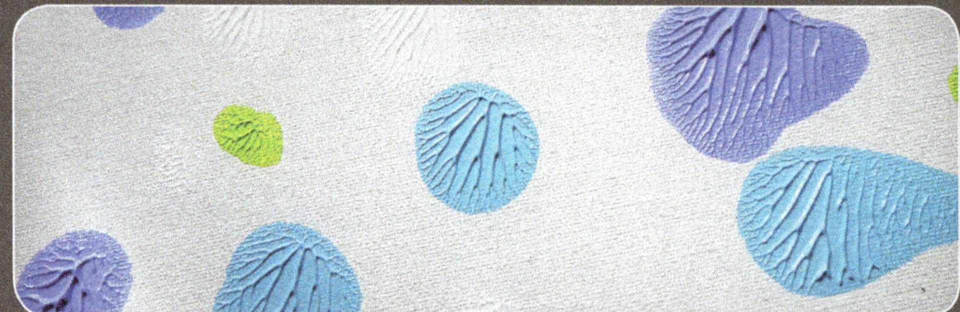

7. Slowly peel the paper away and put it aside to dry. Check out the interesting texture you just created... Beautiful! Don't worry about what anything looks like for now, we are playing and experimenting and your surface is your playground!

8. If you can contain your excitement, let things dry overnight. If not (I know the feeling!), you can use a hair dryer/heat tool. The paint is a little thick so you will need to be patient. Keep in mind that sometimes, the paint looks dry on the surface but can still be wet underneath... To check, gently press one of the dry blobs with your finger: if it doesn't move at all, it is dry but if it feels a little soft then you need to wait a little longer.
Make sure everything is thoroughly dry before proceeding to the next step!

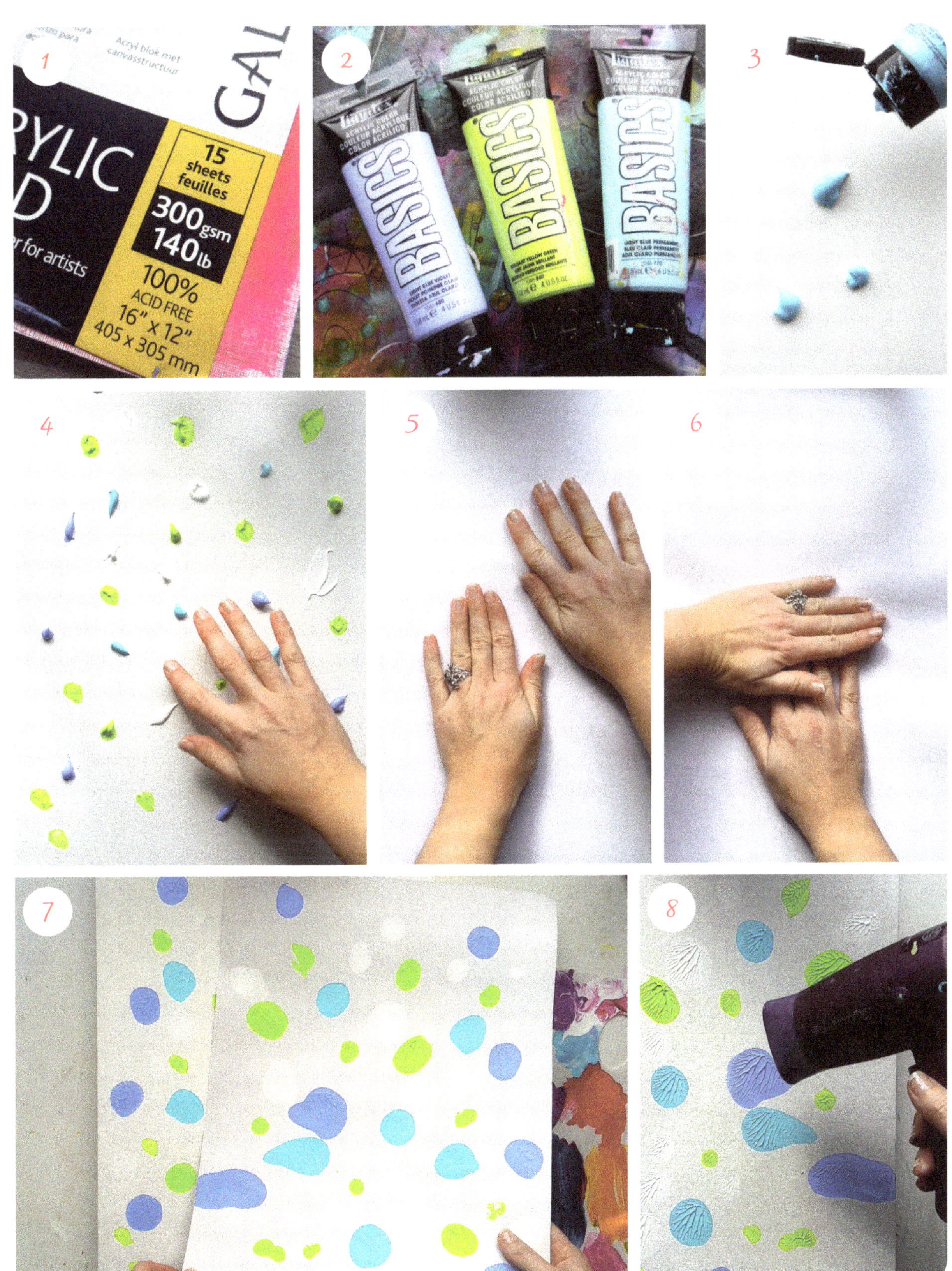

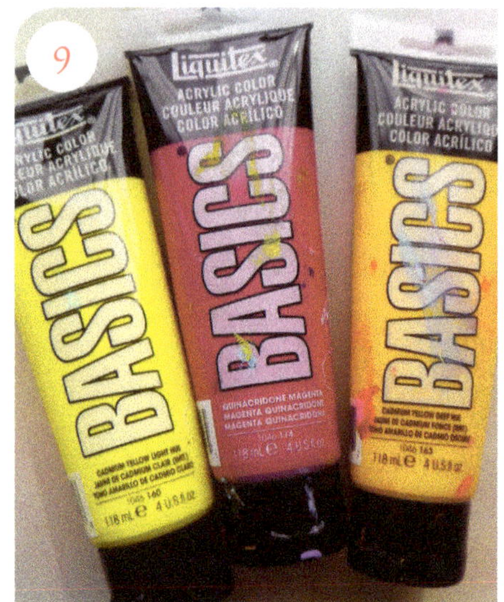

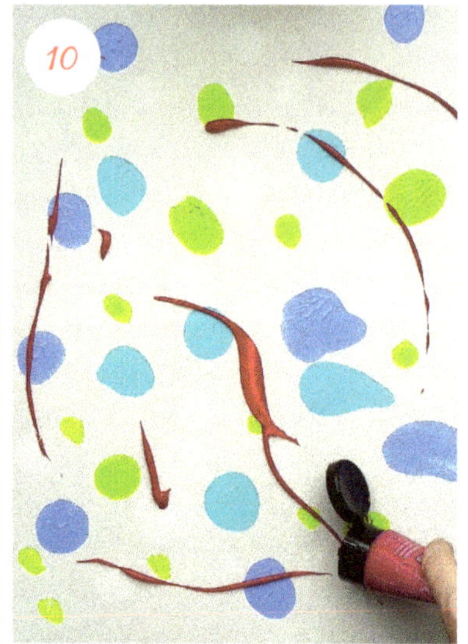

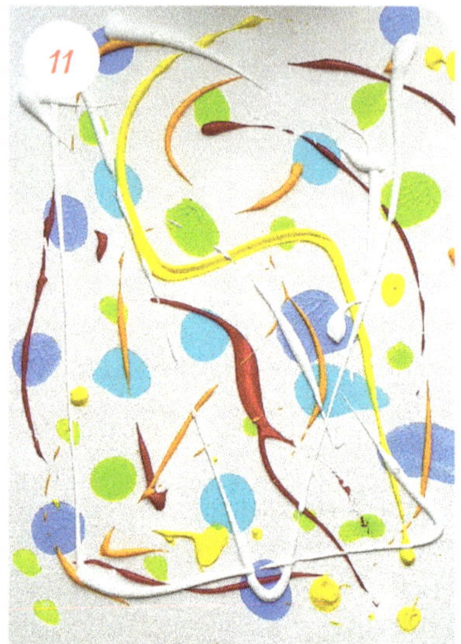

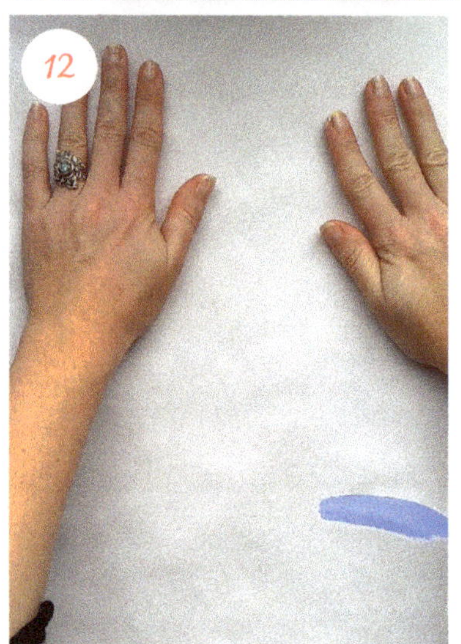

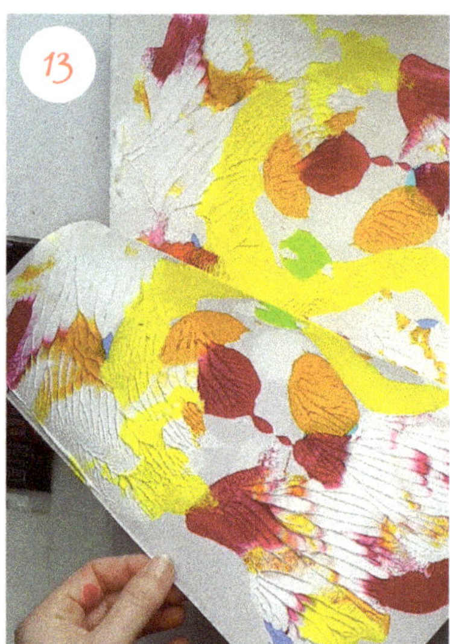

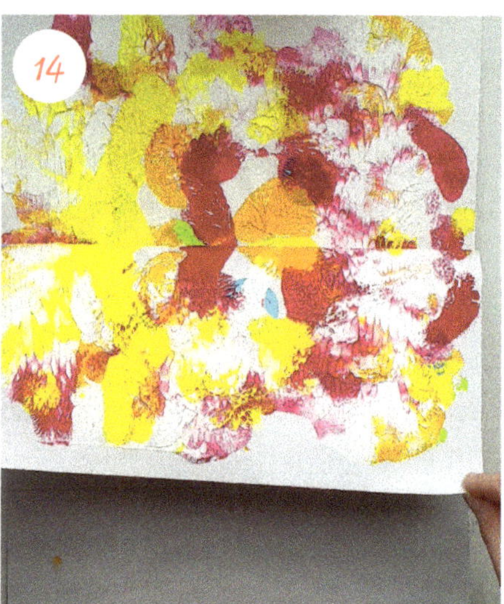

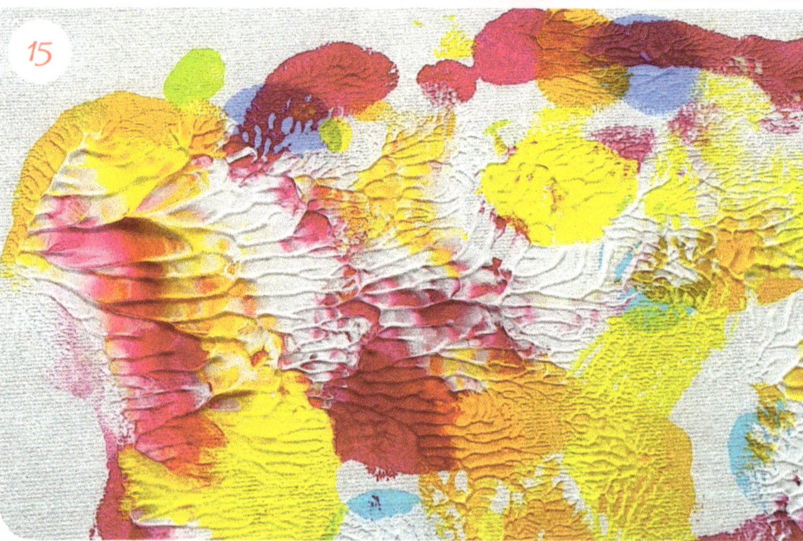

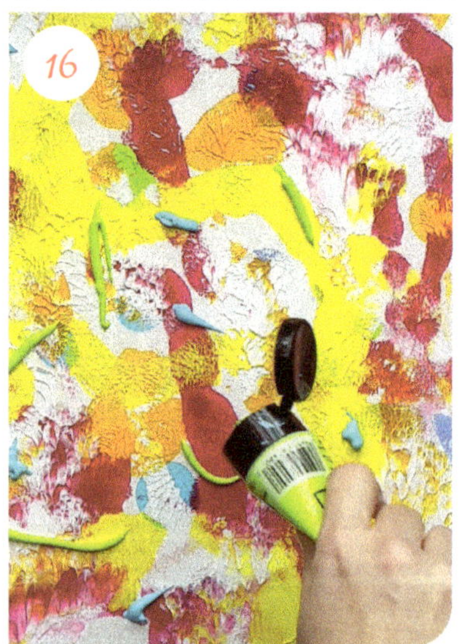

# Let the fun really begin!

**9** Things are going to change dramatically with a second layer!
If you used cool colours for the first one, then now choose warm colours to contrast:
yellow, magenta and orange (or reverse).

**10** Turn up the fun by adding lines of paint, spirals, circles... Whatever tickles your fancy!
No right or wrong way to do this.

**11** Overlap these three new colours with each other and add some white.
Be a bit more generous with the paint this time... The more paint, the thicker the texture!
No need to cover the entire surface as the paint will spread when we 'squish' it.

**12** Now grab the same sheet of paper you used before (it should also be dry) and gently
place it over your surface, face down. As we have more paint than before, you may need
to press and rub a little harder to get the colours underneath to mix as much as possible.
Watch out, they are also more likely to ooze out that this time!

**13** Gently peel the sheet of paper to reveal new awesome texture!

**14** Now turn your wet sheet of paper around (top becomes bottom and vice versa) and
place it back down on your surface (while everything is still wet). Press and rub once
again then peel off... You've got this now, right?

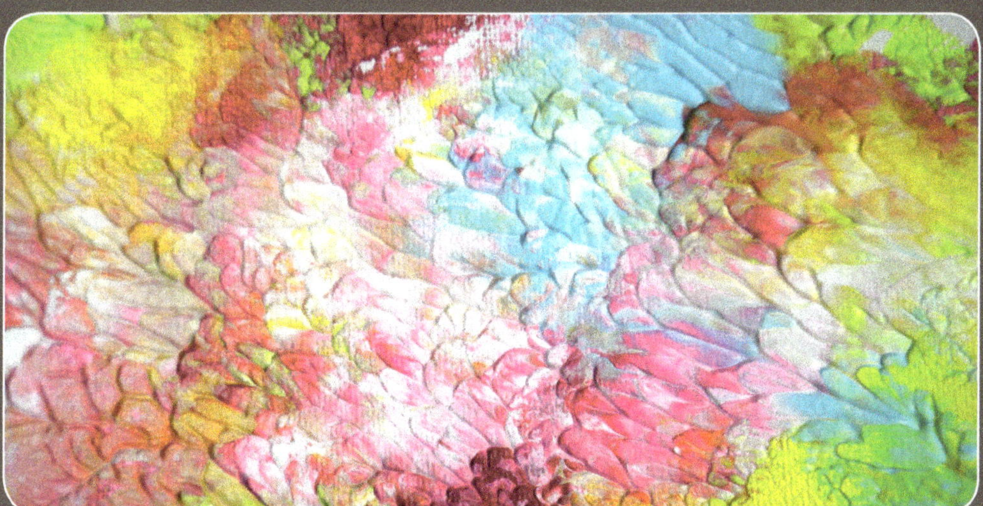

**15** Admire the stunning effect you now have. Isn't it cool?!! Go on, you can say it out loud!

**16** If you have a few unpainted patches, add more paint in the colour(s) of your choice
directly on your surface. I am adding light turquoise and green as those colours don't
stand out enough for me at the moment then...

**17** Repeat the process: place the sheet of paper face down, hold it in place while pressing and 'massaging' the paint underneath. Mhhh, a bit more to the left... Yep, that's the spot! Gently peel off one corner to see how things are going in there...

**18** I could do with even more blue so while I have the corner peeled away, I am just adding a few more blobs on my canvas. Simply adjust the colours and amount of paint depending on what you created (it is exciting to know you can never reproduce two identical paintings!).

**19** Push the corner back down then peel off the opposite corner to check what is there. I decide to add a bit more blue there too and then... You know what to do!

## Two paintings for the price of one

**20** Press - Rub - Peel Off - Say Wow - Repeat until you are happy! If you are concerned about creating muddy colours then do one colour at a time instead of a few and let dry between each layer. Now that you are done, do you realise you have two paintings on the go?? What a productive artist you are!

## Time for a little assessment...

**21** Stand back and ask yourself: do you have interesting texture, is most of your surface covered with paint, do various colours stand out on their own without being over-blended...? If everything looks good then it's time to let your painting(s) dry. It would probably take 5-10 years or so to dry with a heat gun or hair dryer so you had better leave your two paintings alone until the next day.

When you are sure (are you sure? Really, really sure?) that your surface is completely dry (leave the sheet of paper aside for another day), take a moment to gauge what to do next. You now have 'fresh eyes' and may see things differently from yesterday!

Carefully check over your painting to see if there is a colour or two that you would like to bring out more, if there is too much of one colour, if you have any unpainted patches, etc. For example, on mine I notice that yellow is the dominant colour and I would like to bring some of the pink back. I also notice that I have very small patches of a lovely purple, created when the light turquoise and magenta mingled so...

**22** First, I add some pink paint on my finger and rub it on any unpainted spots, and over any area I want to tone down...

**23** Then I add a little purple here and there, always making sure I gently fade out the paint over what is underneath, so it looks like the colours blend in a little where they meet.

**24** Now my painting feels more balanced with less yellow, and more colourful with the added pink and purple (compare with photo nb. 21). Adjust colours to your needs.

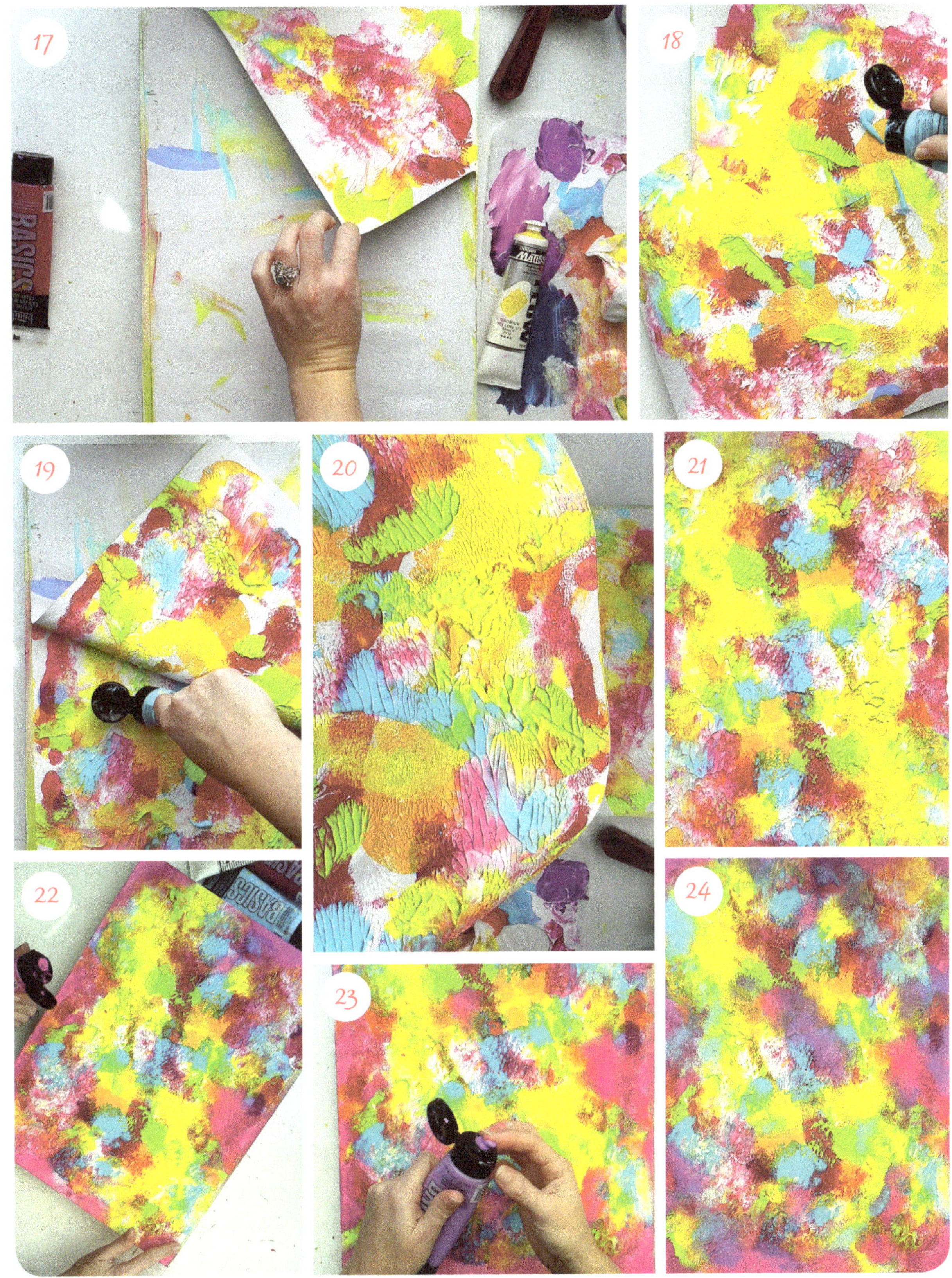

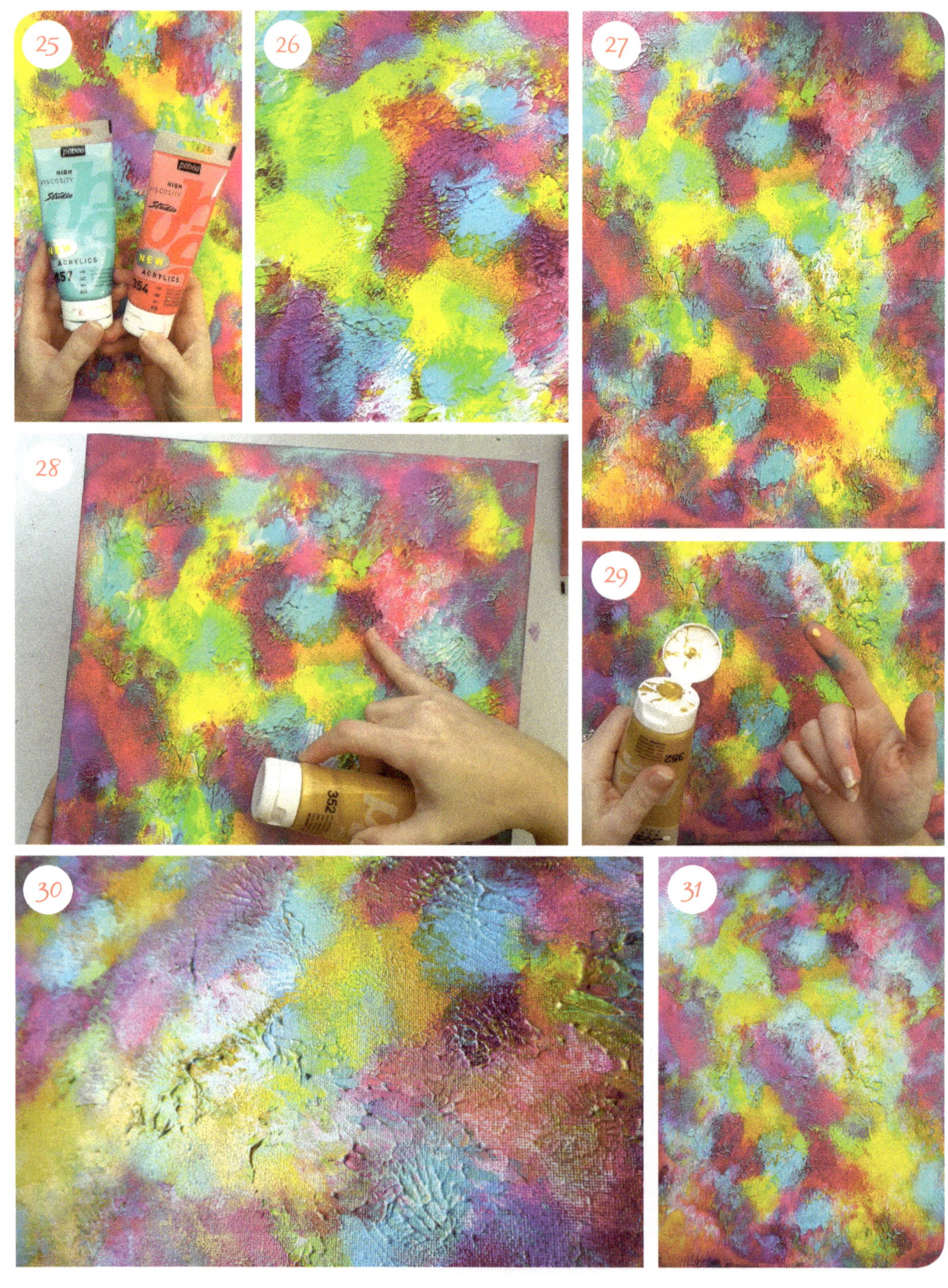

# Metallic iridescent love...

**25**  Optional: There are many things I love in life and one of them is iridescent paint.
I love, love, love the mysterious shine it brings to a painting!
If you do too (you Shiny Soul), then let's turn this painting into something truly special!
If that is not your thing then your painting is finished (and I still love you)!

**26**  Rub a little (or a lot - I am addicted so I will not judge) iridescent 'blue green' mostly over
the blue/green areas and iridescent 'red blue' mostly over the magenta/purple areas.

**27**  Applying iridescent colours over similar colours (such as blue on blue, red on magenta)
allows you to get a subtle shine until light hits the painting and then, WOW!
As an added bonus, iridescent paints will help intensify some of your colours underneath.

**28**  I know it may sound like an overkill but trust me, adding a little light gold paint is really
worth it and looks beautiful over any darker colours like the purple here.

**29**  Put a tiny blob on your finger and 'lightly' rub your finger parallel to your surface.
This will allow you to highlight the raised texture without covering the colours underneath.

**30**  Don't be afraid to use gold to tone down any area where you may have put
too much iridescent paint. Just put a little bit at a time, and repeat!

I like to cover most of my surface with
a little gold, including the edges and
around/over the iridescent paint but I
always do this in thin layers.
Again, gold is optional but if you try it
and don't like it, then just go over with
some of colours used previously, followed
by a little iridescent paint if you wish.

**31**  Either way, the results are just stunning
and this painting now feels really special!
Now you can stand back and loose
yourself into your dreamy painting...

*The finished painting is showcased on page 106*

***

Hey, remember that sheet of paper from
earlier? Here is what I did with it, just to show
you that you don't have to stop here!
I used purple around the edges to create
a very subtle border, added a little shine
(of course!) and a quote I like... Love!

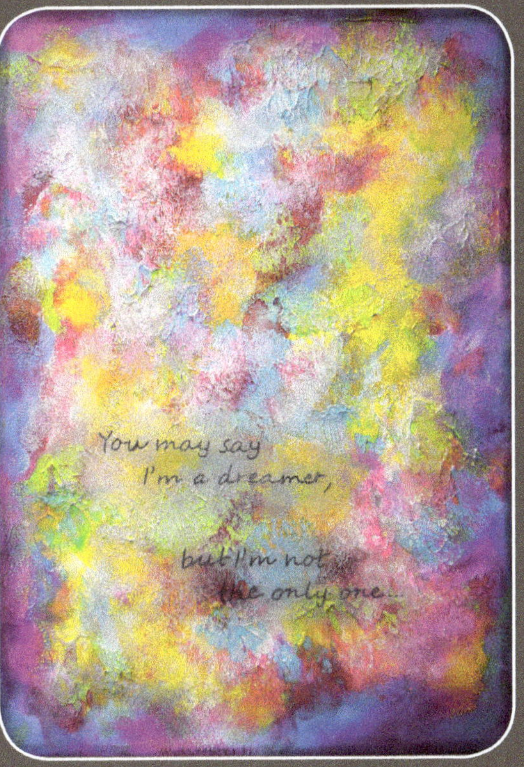

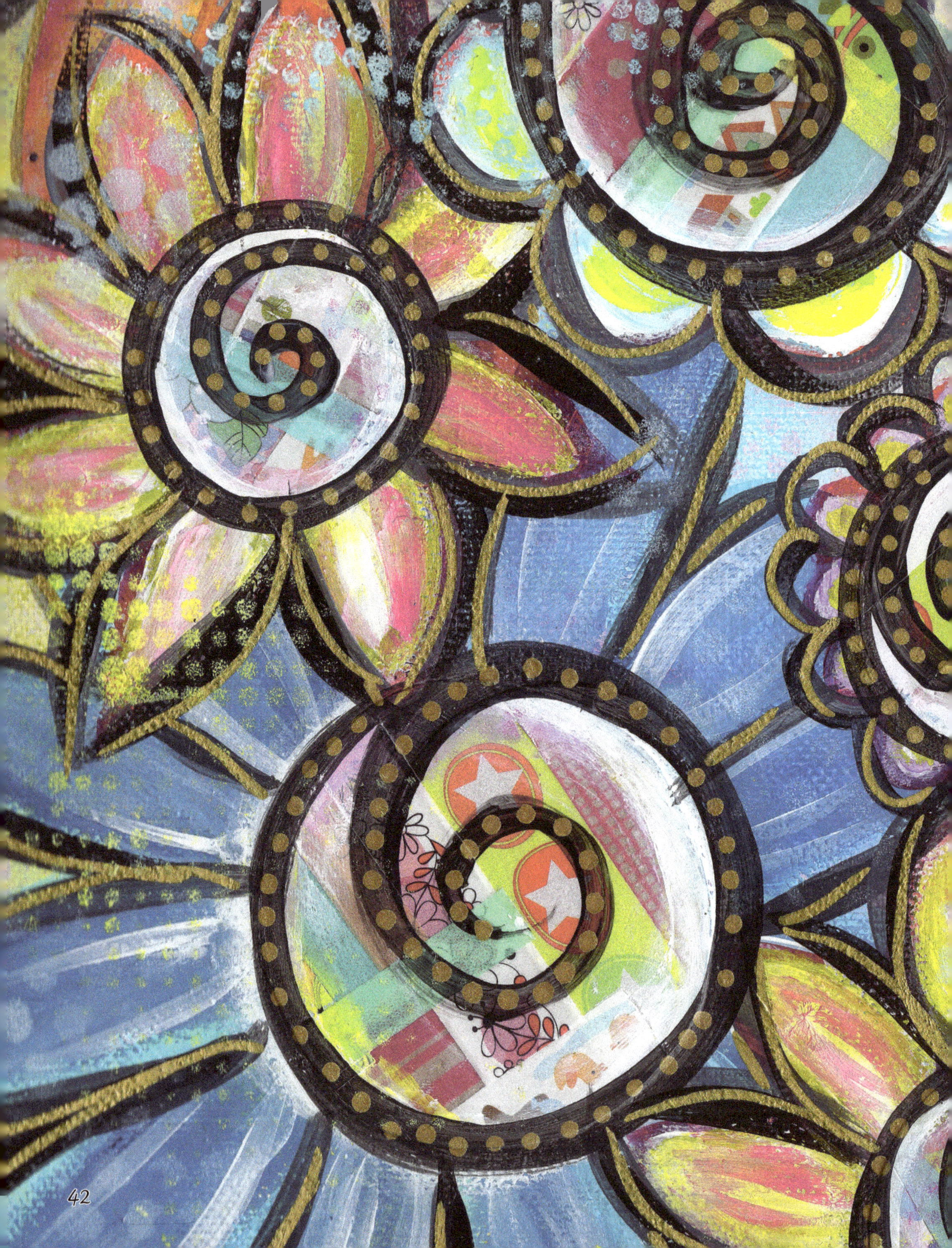

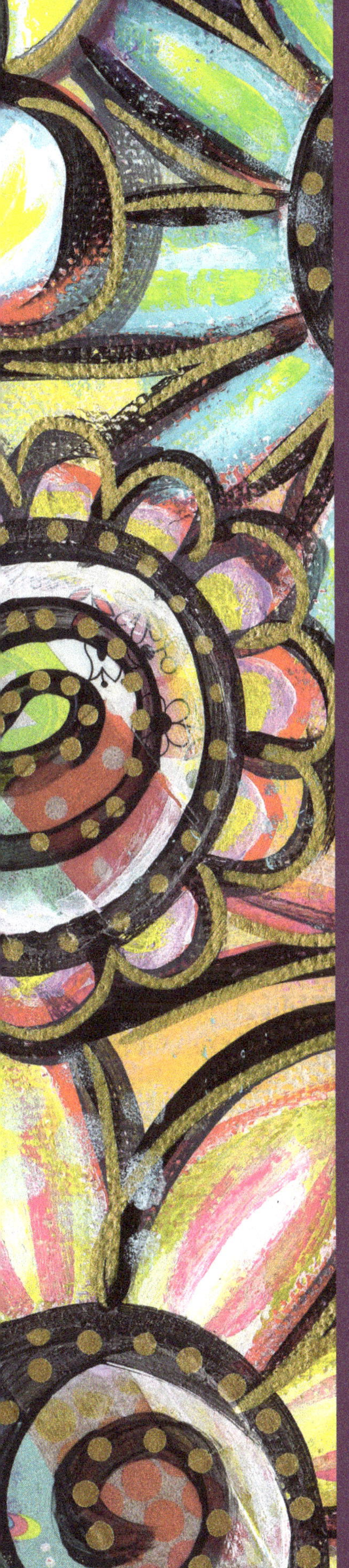



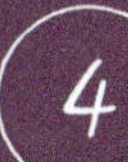

# 4

# Flower Power

## Oh Darling... This is going to be a blast!

Follow me on a new crazy adventure!

First stop will be at *'Raid Your Washi Stash'* to finally put those pretty rolls to good use...

Then we will stop at *'Build a Funky Background'* but once there, we will throw our baggage away and go to an even more exciting destination!

Yes, I know how scary it can be to arrive at a point you feel comfortable with only to let it go, and move on!

But trust me, pushing yourself will make you a stronger artist... And it will make your art even better so, relax, and enjoy the ride!

## Recommended supplies

- Washi tape: 5 strips (or more) about 12 in (30 cm) long in various colours and designs
- Acrylic paint: yellow, lime green, white, magenta, orange, deep turquoise, Prussian blue, red, black, dark purple, light turquoise (or use YOUR favourite colours) + light purple (or add white to dark purple)
- Tim Holtz stencils: 'Bubble' and 'Dot Fade'
- Gold marker pen 1.8-2.5mm
- Gel medium

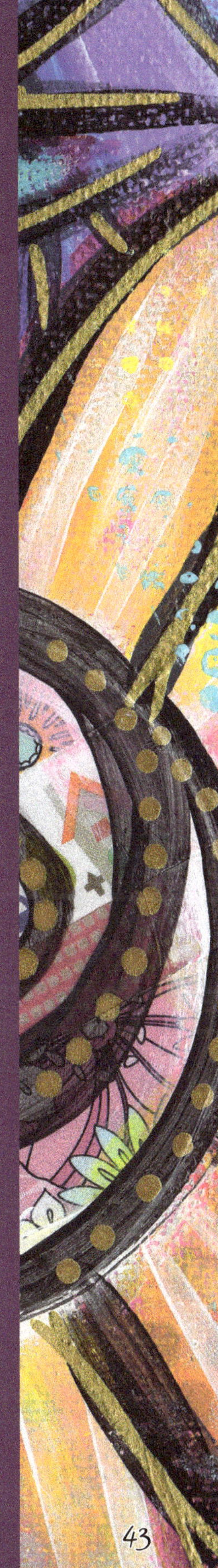

# Washi goodness!

You won't need much washi tape for this project but...
If you don't have/like/want to buy washi tape then you could make your own!

- Cut at least 5 x 12 in (30 cm) long strips of regular masking tape (10 mm wide/0.4 in) & stick
  them on a sheet of uncoated baking/freezer paper, with a little space between each one
- Paint each length of tape in different colours/designs and add marks/doodles on top
- Let dry and you have handmade washi tape!

**1** Select 5 washi tape rolls/strips in various colours, that you feel go reasonably well together.
Of course they will be different from the ones I use here but I know you can adapt yourself!

**2** Cut a piece of thin cardstock big enough to create various large circles (mine is about 15 x
30 cm or 6 x 12 in and I am working on a 30 x 40 cm or 12 x 16 in canvas).
Cut a small length of your first roll/strip (any design of any length) and stick it on your
cardstock. Then repeat, repeat, repeat! Vary the direction of the pieces of tape and
place them side by side (avoid gaps).

**3** When your cardstock piece is covered, you may notice thin gaps here and there. You
can cover them up with thinner strips of washi tape or by cutting one of your strips in half
lengthways. Ensure everything is well stuck down by pressing your finger along each piece.

**4** Use a ball point pen to trace as many circles of various sizes as you can on your tape.
If you don't have a plastic template, use the bottom of paint bottles, a roll of toilet
paper, a glass... Anything you find (and may have already used in a previous chapter!).

**5** Now cut all your circles as neatly as possible.
You will have leftover pieces that you may be able to use in another project!

**6** Arrange the circles on your surface: alternate large and small, leave enough space around
each one and avoid placing them too close to the edges of your surface.
If you have too many circles, select your best ones and keep the rest for later!
Move the circles around so that the strips of washi tape are at slightly different angles.

**7** When you are happy with placement, dip your square wash brush in gel medium.
Lift up one of the circles, spread gel medium on your surface (a bit larger
than the circle) and also on the back of the circle. Press the circle into the wet area
and brush on more gel medium over it and around the edge.
Make sure everything is well covered! Repeat with the remaining circles.

**8** When everything is dry, check if anything is not stuck down properly. If so, dip your
finger/brush in gel medium and apply where needed (over and under). Let dry.

**9** Dip your finger in gesso and 'paint' along the edge of the circles (don't be afraid
to put a little bit over the edge of the washi tape as we will paint a little over it later on).

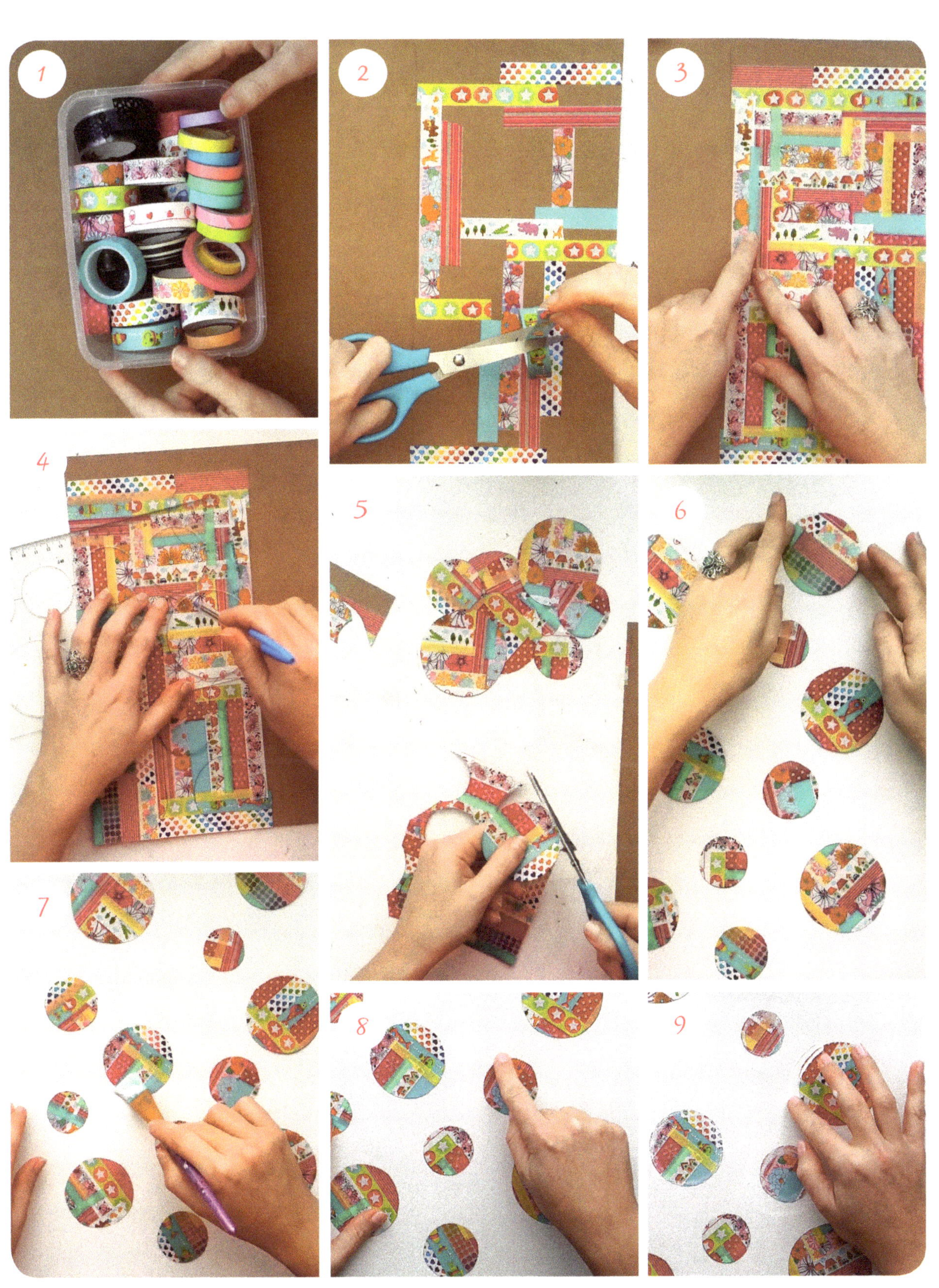

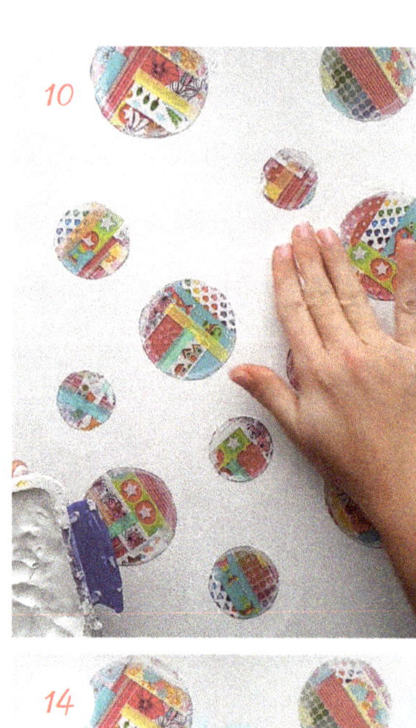

10

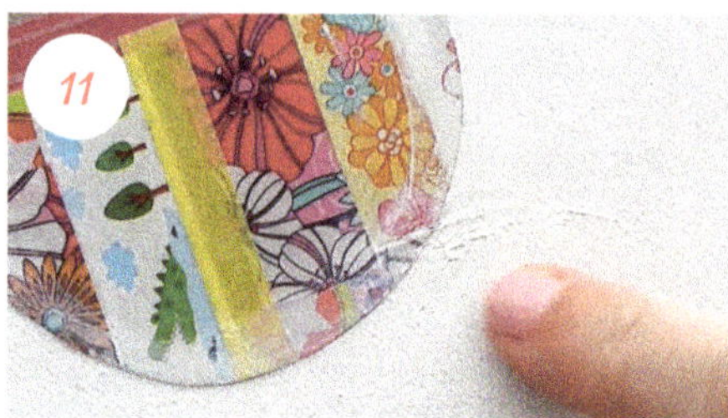

11

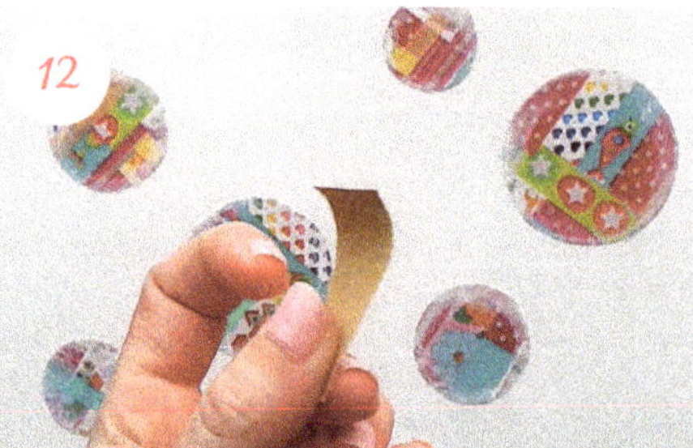

12

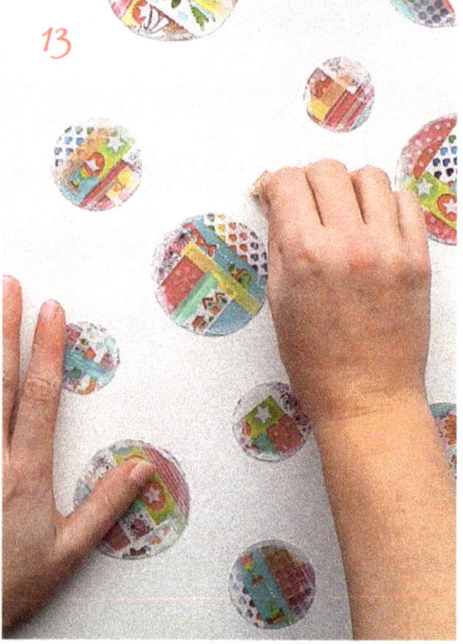

13

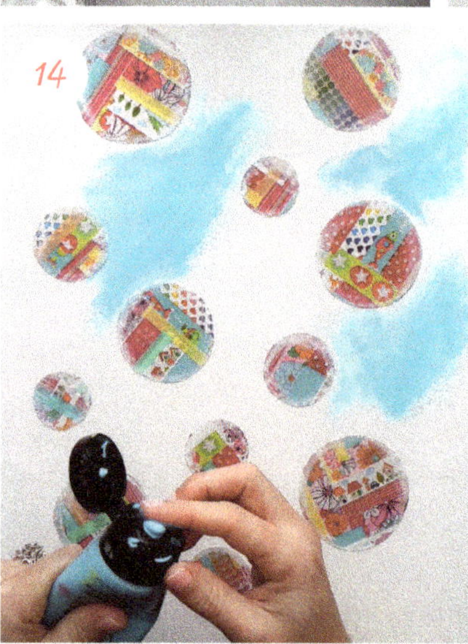

14

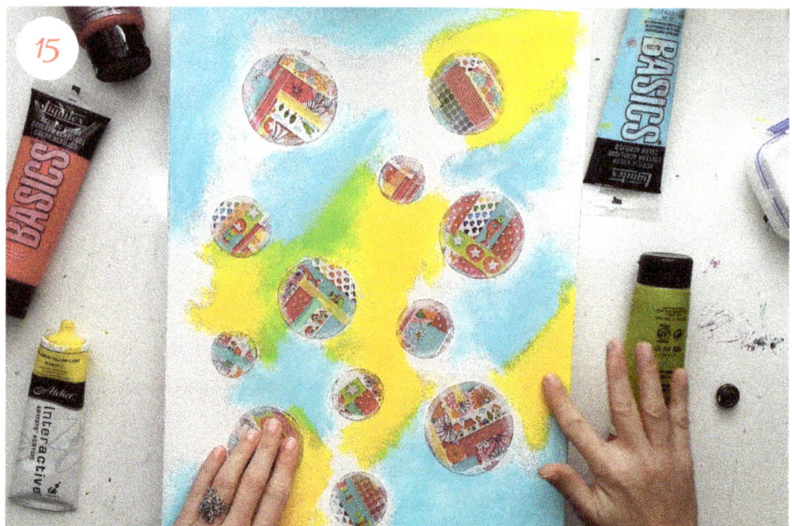

15

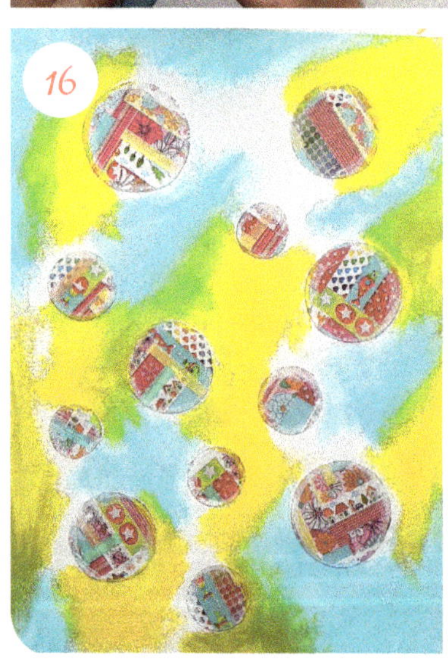

16

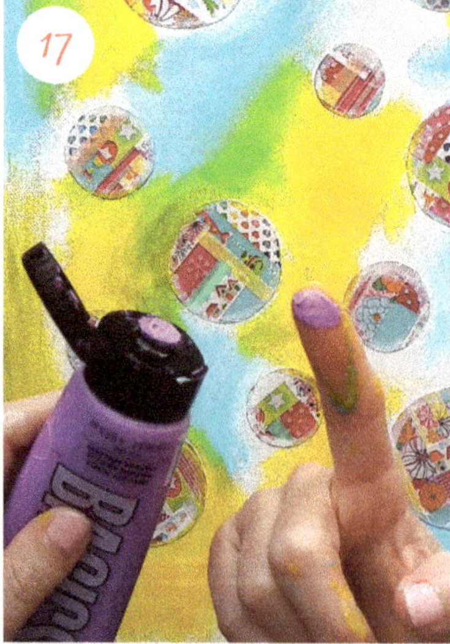

17

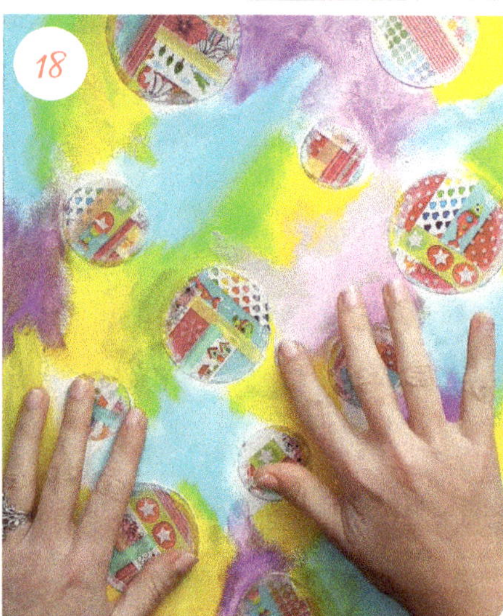

18

**10** Optional: If you are using a canvas/board then it is most likely already primed with gesso. I like to apply my own so I know exactly what is on my surface but this is not necessary! If you decide to do the same then dip your finger(s)/brush in gesso and spread it in a circular motion around the circles. Let dry.

## Made a little mess?  No problem!

**11** Inspect your surface up close and if you discover a few marks left by the application of the gel medium or gesso, then don't worry, they can be easily fixed!

**12** Tear off a tiny (and I do mean tiny!) piece of fine grade sanding paper from a larger piece...

**13** ... And gently rub the sanding paper over the offending areas, until smooth to the touch (don't worry if it looks like they are still there as they will get covered). Wipe the 'dust' away.

**14** Pick a colour that repeats in some of your washi tape (light turquoise for me) and squeeze a little paint straight onto your finger. Rub it on your surface and create a few patches.

**15** Repeat with a second colour (yellow for me)...

**16** ... Then a third (lime green for me). Let everything dry.

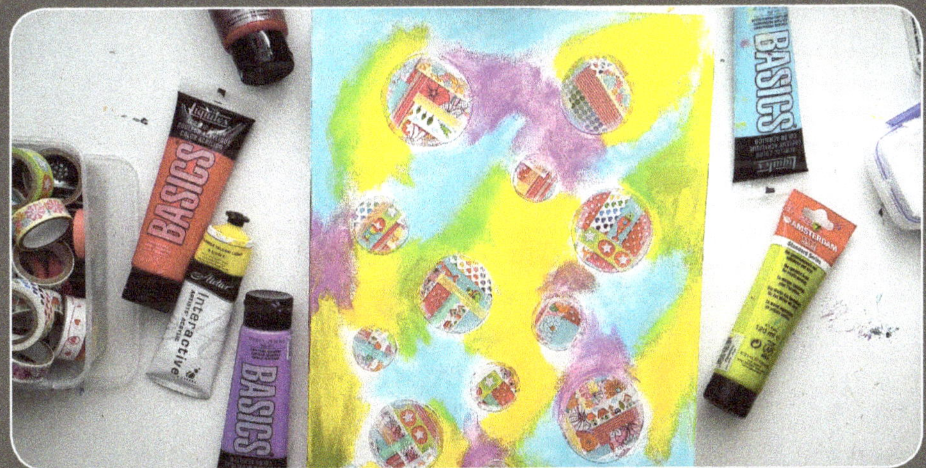

**17** Find a fourth colour (light purple for me) and fill in the remaining unpainted areas. No need to put more than this much on your finger as it is easier to spread the paint in thin layers. Let dry.

## Softening things up...

**18** Now mix a little gesso (or white paint) and purple straight onto your surface and blend partly over a yellow/green patch. The goal here is to tone down the existing purple.

**19**   Now use a little white paint to 'soften up' some of the larger areas of colour. Scan your painting for a flat area of colour (like my blue corner here), rub a little white over it (but not all over it!), in a circular motion. This helps create very subtle shades of blue...

**20**   Repeat this toning down process with a little white paint over any other flat areas. Note how this simple trick has helped softening up the overall look of your painting!

## Bringing sexy back!

**21**   Let's incorporate some of the colours of your washi tape into your background... Mine has some pink in it, so I am mixing my own shade of pink by adding white to magenta. Let's face it, we don't need to own every single colour under the sun! It is very easy, and satisfying, to be able to create colours you can't get from the shops. Simply mixing two colours together can give you a huge range of gorgeous shades!

**22**   Use any strong colours sparingly and as a way to create a little highlight around part of the circles.

**23**   Don't be afraid to add a little white as you go along if the colour is still too strong.

**24**   Repeat with another colour from your washi tape. In my case, the same light turquoise used in the background...

**25**   ... Then purple, pink , white again if needed. It is up to you how intense you want your colours to be! Don't be shy and play, adapt your colours to the ones of your washi tape. I know it may seem like we are going back and forth (and we are!) but it is fun and relaxing to blend and move the paint around, isn't it? I promise there is a purpose to all this!

Keep going until you are happy with the result.
If you aren't, take a break from your painting while everything is drying and just walk away!
Come back to it later on (or even the next day) and assess what is not working for you...

Do you have too much of one colour?
Is one colour too strong compared to the rest?
Do some of the patches of colour need to be softer? Etc...

Try not to judge yourself harshly and modify your painting until you are happy.
Things could change rapidly very soon (hint, hint) so there is no need to worry!

It may not feel like your painting has changed much but if you compare mine in this photo with photo nb. 20, can you see how some depth was created, along with subtle shadows and highlights? It was worth it!

**26**   Now it is time to add a little texture with two of my favourite stencils, 'Bubble' and 'Dot Fade' by Tim Holtz. I recommend them to you because they are 'generic' enough to use in any background, and the results can be as subtle or strong as you like.

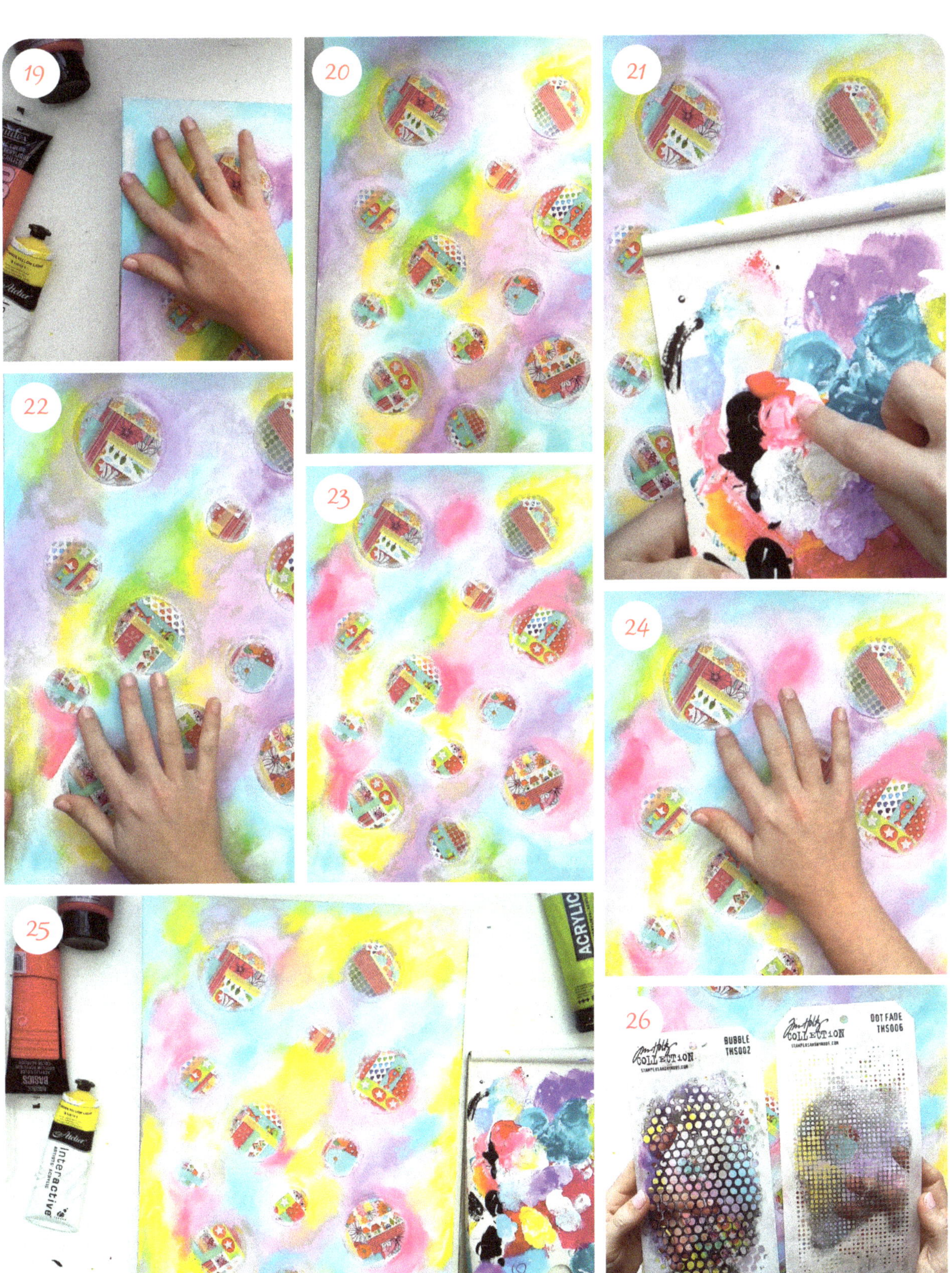

19
20
21
22
23
24
25
26
BUBBLE
THS002
DOT FADE
THS006
COLLECTION
STAMPLESLADYMARY.COM
ACRYLIC

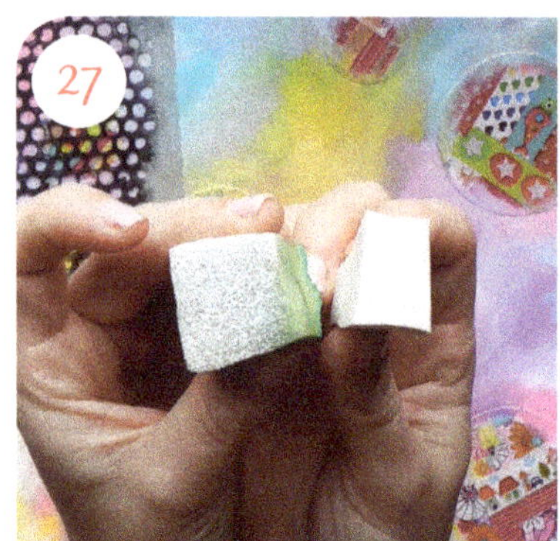

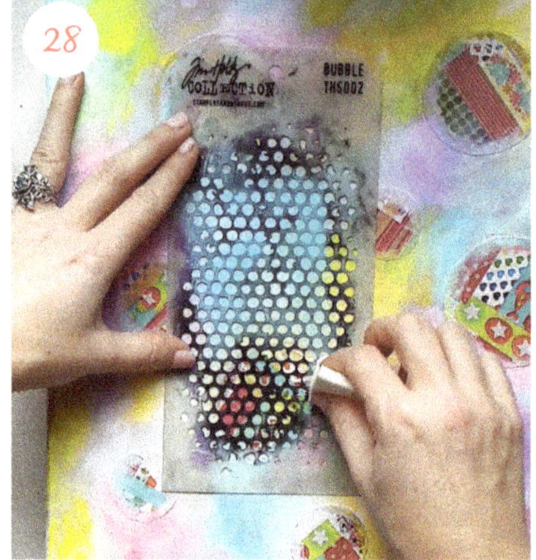

Tim Holtz
COLLECTION
BUBBLE
THS002


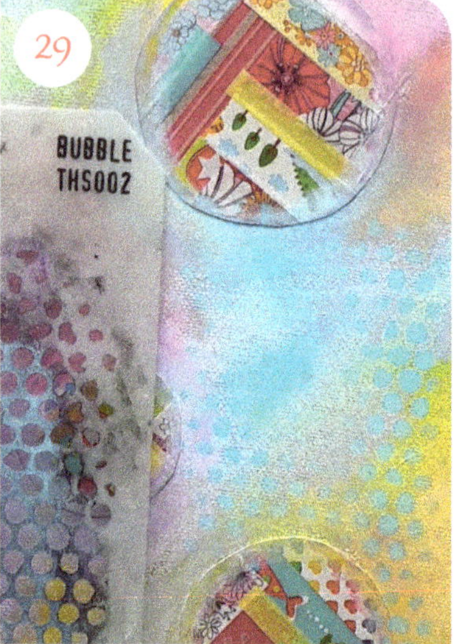

BUBBLE
THS002


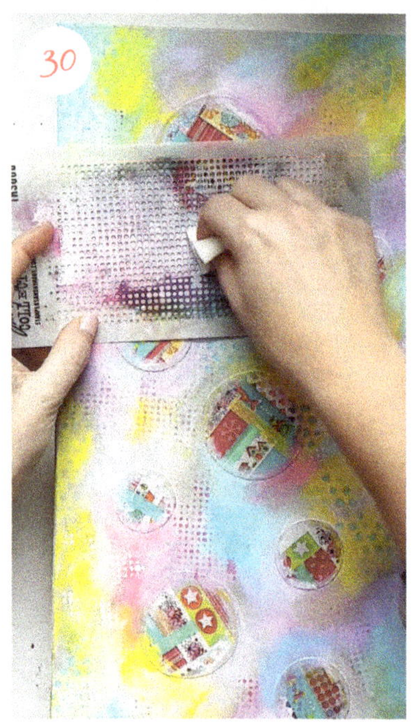

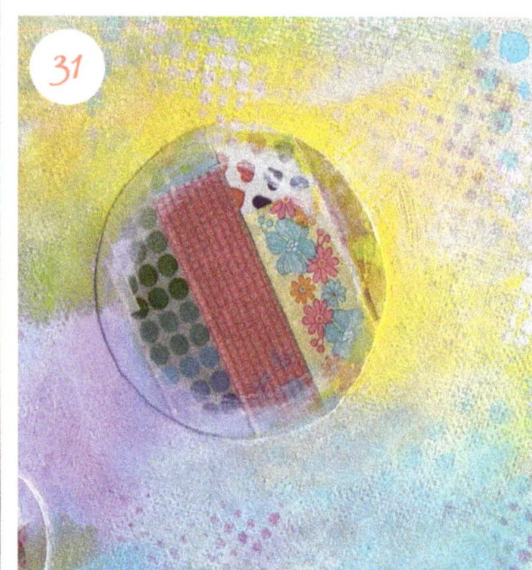

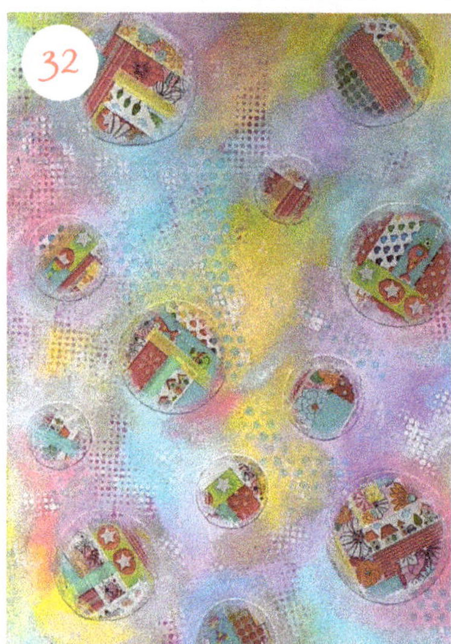

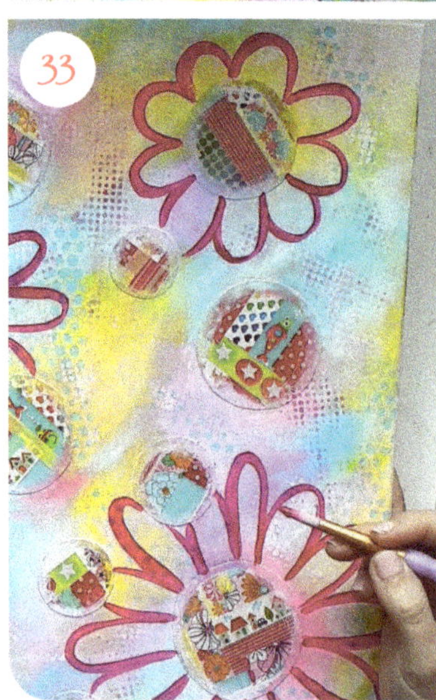

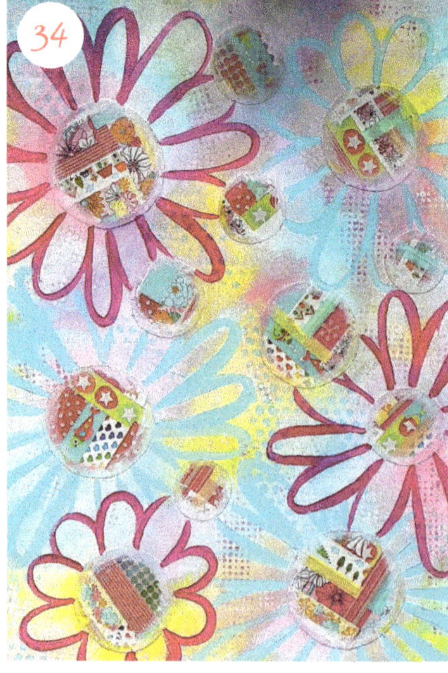

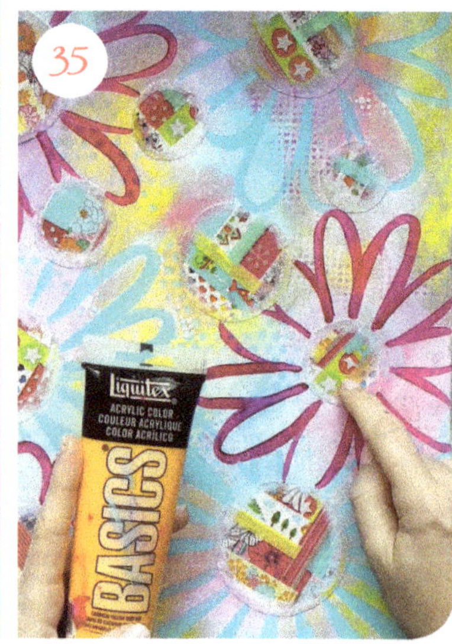

Liquitex
ACRYLIC COLOR
COULEUR ACRYLIQUE
COLOR ACRILICO
BASICS

**27** As you know by now, the easiest way to add paint through a stencil is with a little foam/latex makeup sponge or a little piece of kitchen sponge, but you could also use a stipple brush... Grab whatever you have available!

**28** Use a colour you already used in previous layers (in my case light turquoise), just so everything ties in. Dab your sponge over the 'Bubble' stencil, always up and down and with hardly any paint to avoid seepage.

**29** Dabbing the turquoise over yellow (where it contrasts), into the existing turquoise (where it disappears), gives the illusion that the blue bubbles are slowly fading... Experiment with this easy 'gradient' effect by varying the pressure of your sponge and stencilling one colour over another!

**30** Now use a clean or new sponge and the 'Dot Fade' stencil with a little magenta and white, without mixing the colours together (they will mix as you stencil).

**31** Add a little more pink in some areas and a little more white in others without cleaning your sponge in between to get a lovely variation of shades.

**32** I think you will agree when I say your painting suddenly looks a lot more interesting now! Adding a little texture has given it more depth. It looks pretty cool, if I may say so myself! At this point you could stop and add doodles, write inspiring words or a quote around the circles for example and that would be great!

BUT, can you push yourself and let go of the work you have just created...? Of course, you can! I know it is not easy and it takes a little courage - believe me, I have been there! Every now and then, I get to a stage where I am happy with my creation but something tells me it could be better. I hesitate because I am scared to ruin what I have done (and don't want to feel like it was a waste of time). But each time I have pushed past my fears, my paintings have ALWAYS improved! And in turn I have always felt stronger for being brave. And so, I sincerely encourage you to take that scary step as it will make you grow as an artist! Don't think about it, just do it :-)

## Time to be courageous!

**33** Dip a fine tip brush (I am using a size 8) in a colour that will stand out (magenta for me), and draw large petals around three of your larger circles, preferably away from each other. Keep your wrist loose to avoid creating anything too neat! When you get near an unpainted circle, make your petals go 'behind' it  to create the illusion  that one circle is front of the other.

**34** Repeat the same process with another contrasting colour (light turquoise for me) and paint three other large circles, preferably away from each other, just to create a little balance in your painting. Again, make the blue petals go 'behind' the pink ones and the other unpainted circles, so it will look like the blue flowers are in the background... Let dry.

**35** Look at the colours you have on your washi tape and see if there is one that you may not have used yet, such as this orange for me.

**36** Add a blob of orange paint to your palette and have some gesso handy. Dip your finger in orange and fill in your first petal (select any of the larger pink flowers). Add a little gesso to the orange as you go along if you wish to make the paint more opaque and less 'flat'.

**37** This photo shows how I made some petals more opaque than others so the texture from previous layer is still a little visible. Make sure you go over the pink outlines at little on purpose! Neat freaks: be gone!

**38** Select another large pink flower, and repeat the process with a lighter or different pink (or mix some white to magenta). You want to be able to still see most of the outlines but not completely.

**39** Repeat the process with some yellow and gesso on your last large pink flower. Let dry.

## How to add simple highlights

**40** Dip your finger in a tiny bit of pink and lightly drag it from the centre of the flowers towards the end of the petals (stop just before the end). This creates a 'dry brush' effect! Make the highlights a bit more obvious on some petals than others to create interest, and make sure you don't cover everything up! On the flower you painted orange, add pink highlights.

**41** On the one you painted pink, add yellow highlights.

**42** And on the yellow flower... Add some orange highlights.

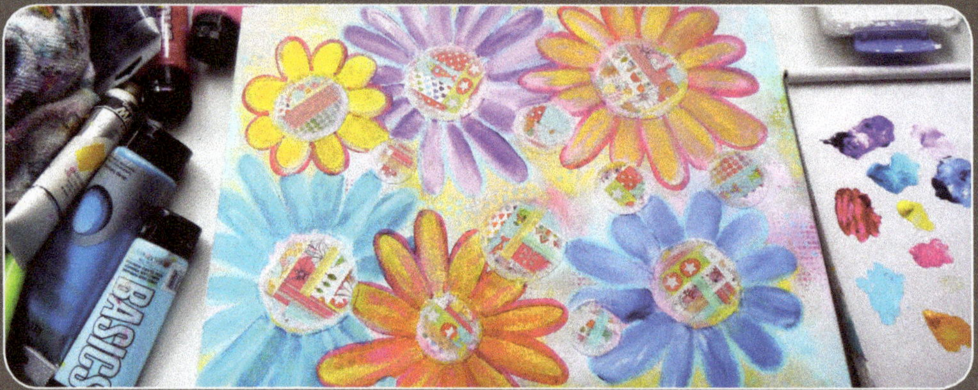

**43** If you used warm colours (yellow, orange, pink) on the previous flowers, it would be great to now use cool colours to make the blue flowers 'recess' in the background (or reverse if you started with cool colours). Let's start with some deep turquoise for the first flower, adding a little gesso here and there for texture and interest, just like you did earlier.

**44** My next flower will now be filled with dark purple and a little gesso...
And the last flower in the top right of my canvas will be filled with some Prussian blue and a little gesso. Remember to go over the outlines a little without covering them completely.

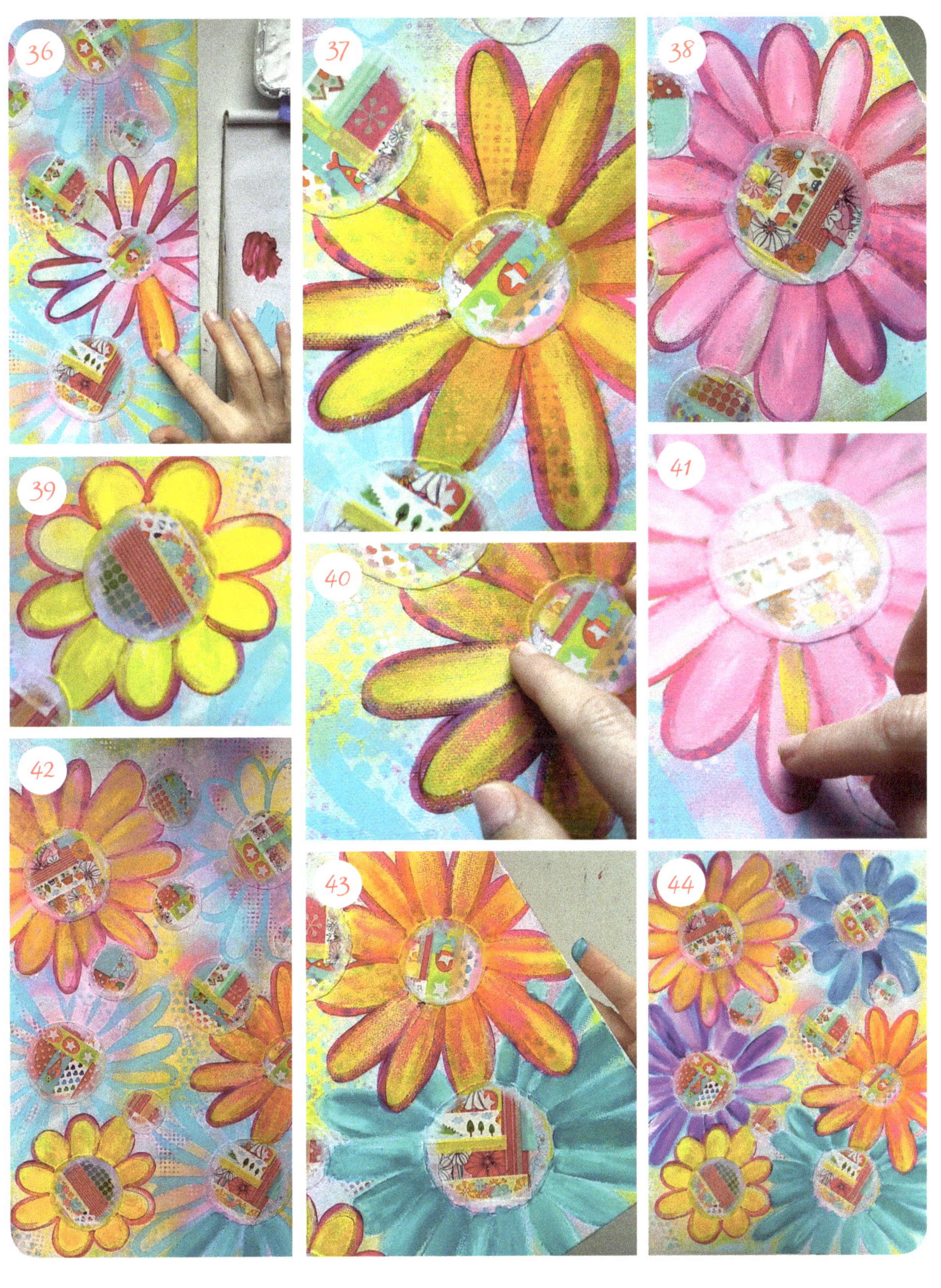

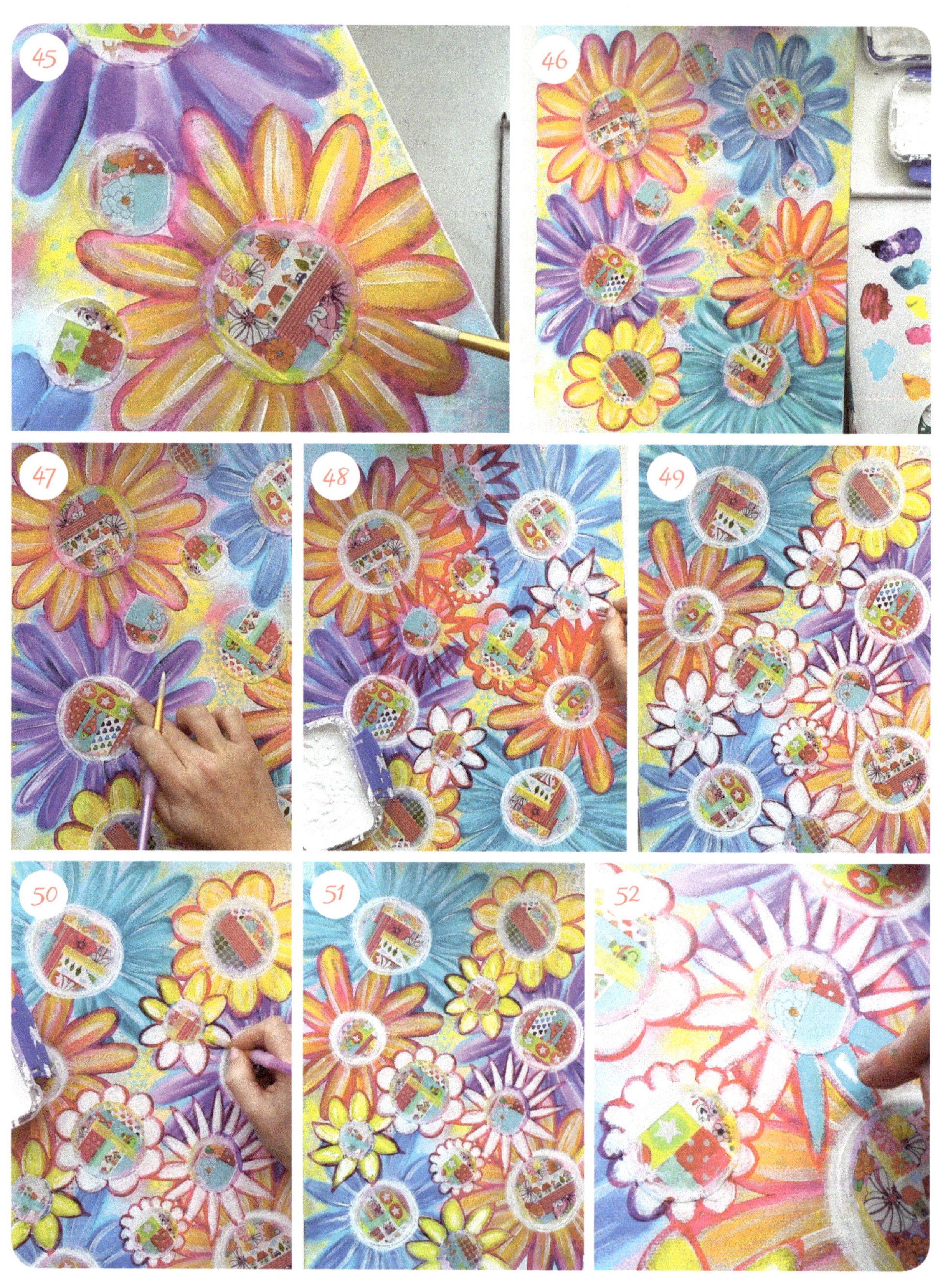

# A few more highlights...

**45** Let's zing things up with some white highlights! Dip your fine tip brush into white paint (or gesso) and create thin, loose lines: drag your brush from the edge of the circle towards the tip of the petals - lift up your brush just before you get to the outline. The 'lifting up' will prevent hard edges on the end of your white lines.

**46** Repeat on every single flower you have on your surface! Experiment with changing the pressure of your brush a little to vary your highlights. Add one line on some petals, two on others, soften up some of them with your finger. It is a quick process once you get in the flow!

**47** Now dip the same brush in gesso and paint over the inner and outer edge of each circle. Soften up the wet gesso by rubbing your finger around the edge of the circles. This will prepare the surface for future highlights...

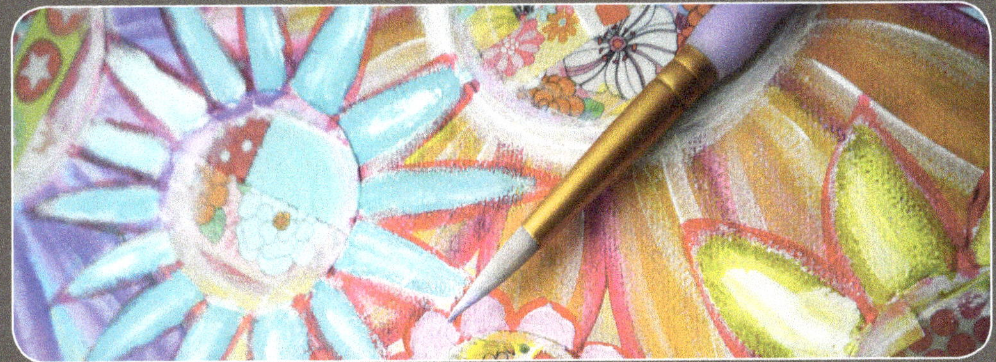

# Onto our small flowers...

**48** Have another look at the colours in your washi tape: is there a bold colour you haven't used much yet? If not, just pick one that will contrast well with everything else (red for me). Draw small petals of various shapes on your smaller unpainted circles, using your fine tip brush. Let dry.
Then fill in the smaller petals with gesso (easier with a brush than finger this time!) to make the petals opaque. This will make our smaller flowers 'stand out' from the background as if they were on top of the larger flowers.

**49** Add another coat of gesso if needed and let everything dry.

**50** Back to your washi tape... Pick a colour in there you haven't used yet (lime green for me). Use your brush to fill in a few of the smaller flowers.

**51** As you did before, rub a little gesso here and there with your finger, to add subtle colour variations and highlights.

**52** Pick another colour (such as turquoise) to fill in one of the small flowers, again with a little gesso. Don't worry about being neat, we will tidy everything up at the end!

**53** Keep painting the petals of your smaller flowers using colours from your washi tape. You could also just add white to previous colours used to create new shades. Here I painted one flower with light blue (Prussian blue mixed with white) and added white gesso highlights. Then I painted the other one with light pink (magenta with white).

**54** Add a little more depth and interest by painting lines on the smaller flowers, the same way you did earlier (start from the edge of the circle, drag and lift up at the end)... Highlights should always be in a contrasting colour to stand out. For me, that will be yellow on the turquoise flower and lime green on the pink flower.

**55** Yellow on the light Prussian blue flower...

**56** And pink over the lime green flower.

**57** I am not really concerned with being neat and neither should you!

**58** Add a little gesso on the inner and outer edges of the circles so all of them now have a white border (just like in step 48). Let dry.

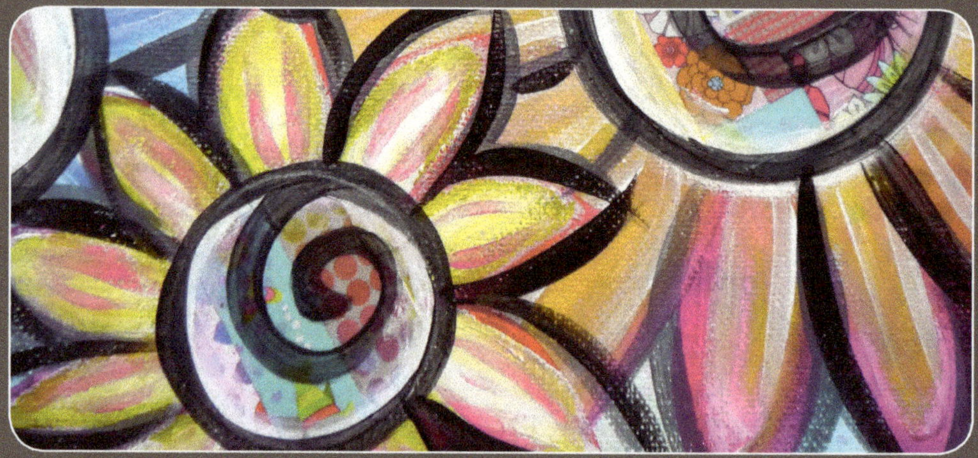

## How to make your flowers pop!

**59** To create even more depth and make our flowers stand out a little, let's now focus on the outlines of the petals: mix a little white paint with black to create a dark grey and loosely go over the outlines of every flower. Drag your fine tip brush from the center to the tips, lifting your wrist up at the end of each stroke. Don't follow your outlines exactly, just use them as a guide. Pretend you can't see properly :-)

**60** Wow, what a difference this has made!!

**61** Now make the center of your flowers pop with spirals! Dip your fine tip brush in dark grey paint and go around the edge of one circle (and slightly over the washi tape). When you arrive back where you started, keep your line going towards the center and create a loop.

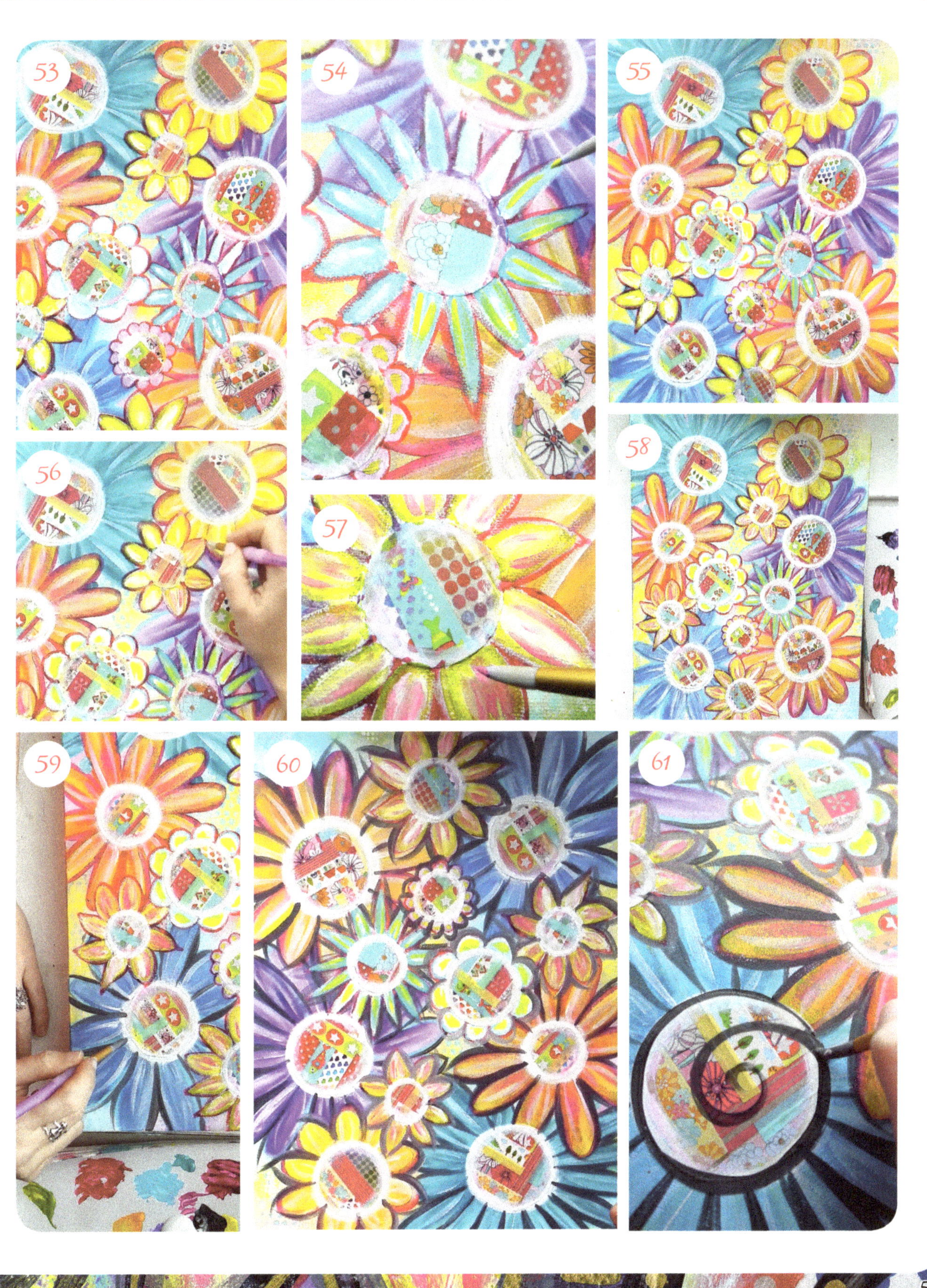

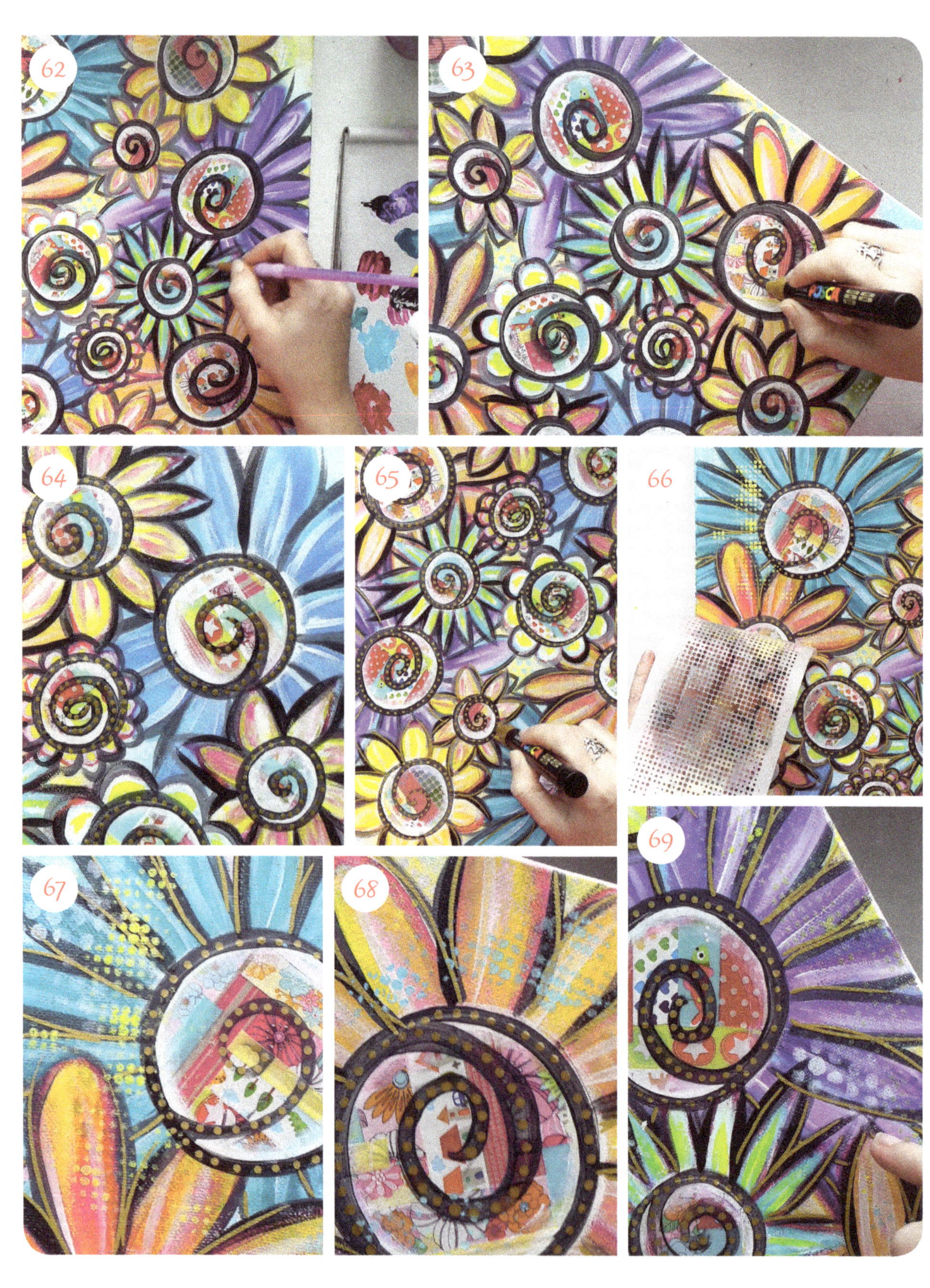

**62** Repeat the process on the center of each flower. The spirals really pop, don't they?! To make some of the flowers stand out a little from the others, loosely outline them with a little black paint. This will add subtle contrast so not ALL the flowers jump at you at the same time! Let dry.

## At last... The finishing touches!

One of my favourite ways to finish a painting is to add little dots over the thick lines. It is a very simple technique that will bring your painting from 'meh' to 'hell yeah'!! I often add white dots but as the background is quite busy here, gold would be a more subtle option.

**63** Grab your large tip gold marker, shake it well, then press the nib a few times on your palette first (you could also use a fine tip brush and gold paint for similar results). Add dots to a spiral.

**64** Vary the pressure of your pen or brush to create different size dots: make them fat where your lines are thick and small on thinner lines.

**65** Repeat the process on every spiral. Avoid smudges by turning your surface around for easier access and if needed, by doing one area at a time, letting the dots dry in between.

**66** Do you remember the texture we added earlier the stencils? I know, I made you cover it up almost completely! But aren't you glad you pushed yourself?! Will you forgive me if I show you how I 'link' my top layers with the previous ones? OK: to do that I simply bring back some of the elements and/or colours I used earlier. Let's try it out...
Choose a warm contrasting colour (yellow for me) to stencil over the 'cool' flowers (for me: Prussian blue, turquoise, purple). Stencil through parts of your 'Dot Fade' stencil and lift one corner to check you are happy. Repeat over your darker colours on the whole surface.

**67** Create some interest by varying the pressure of your sponge so some of the dots will be lighter in colour than other (the more uneven the better!).

**68** Repeat the process but this time, with a cool colour (light turquoise for me) over your warm colours (pink/yellow/orange for me).

**69** Now use your 'Bubble' stencil to add subtle white texture a little here then stand back and shout 'YAY - I'M SO AWESOME!!' - Because YOU. ARE. DONE!

*The finished painting is showcased on page 107*

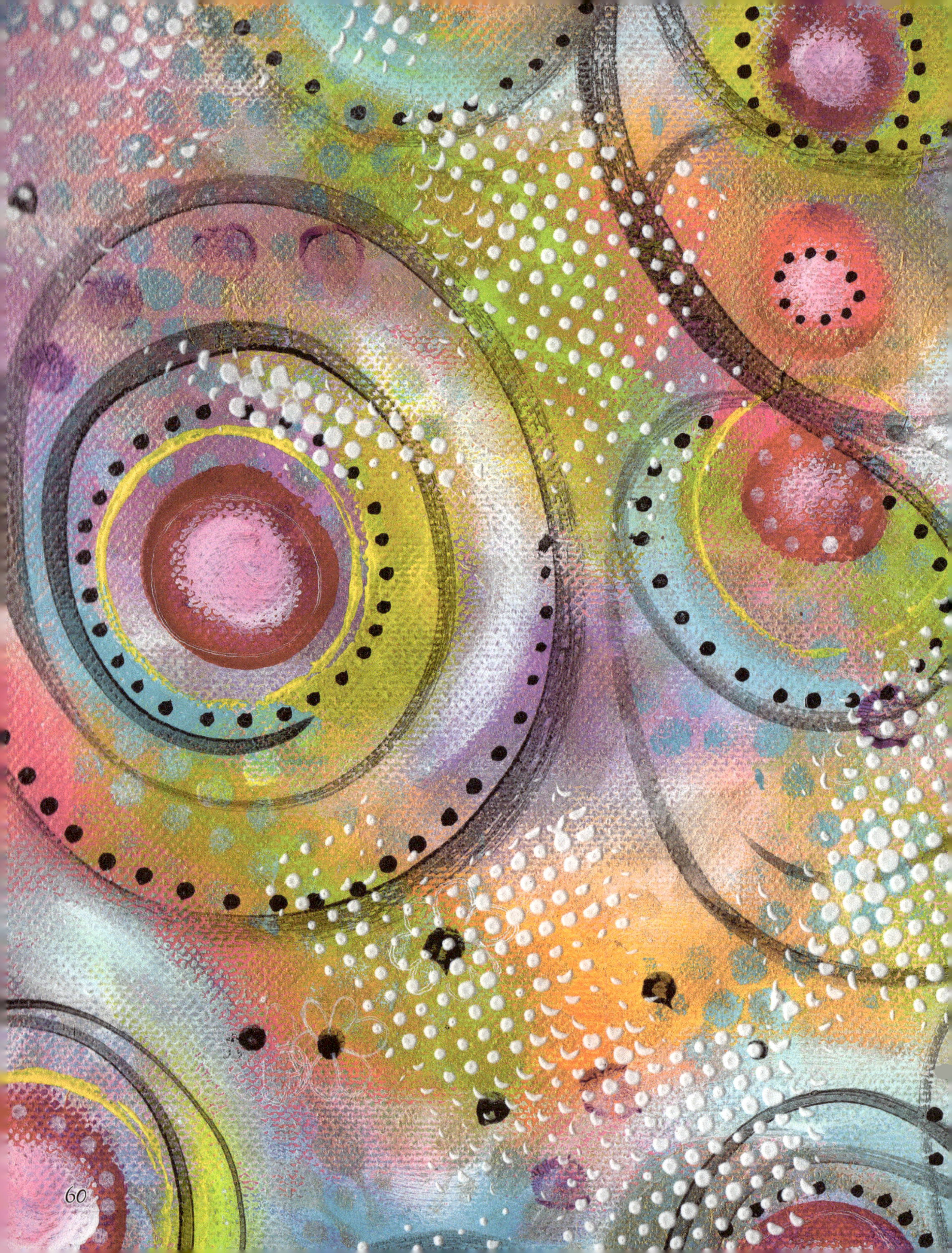

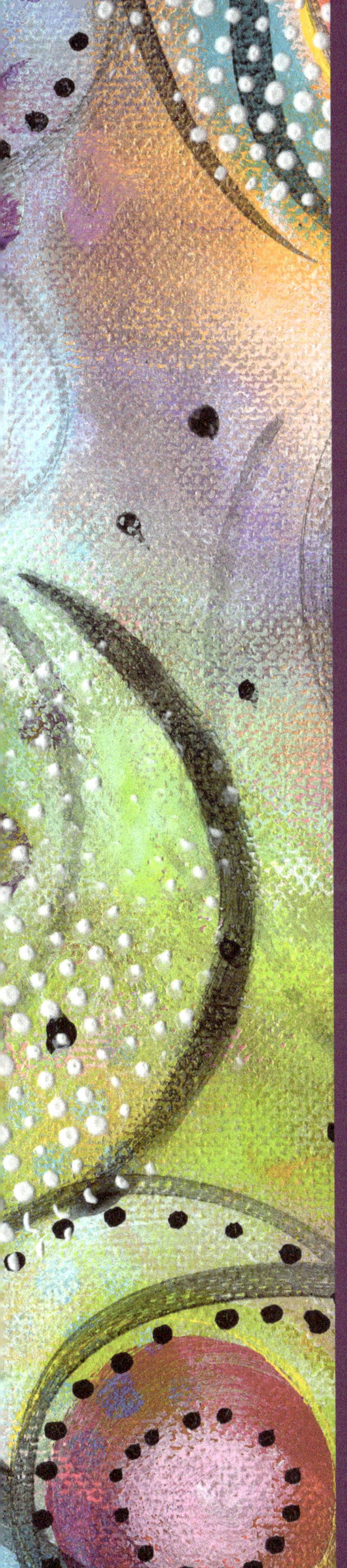

# A Taste of Summer

## Round and round we go!

This is a style of painting I truly love because you really can't go wrong with it. The vibrant colours we are going to use together create a fresh and fun palette that is bound to make you feel happy!

A big focal point is not always needed in a painting. In this chapter I will show you how to create several focal points, forcing you to embrace the painting as a whole.

As circles have always been powerful symbols for a lot of people (I add them everywhere in my art), we will use them to create energy and bounce, with various mediums and tools.

The end result reminds me of mountains of colourful ice-cream! Yum, yum...
I know you know what I mean...!

## Recommended supplies

- Acrylic paint: magenta, orange, yellow, deep turquoise, lime green, white
- Stencils: 'Bubble' and 'Dot Fade' by Tim Holtz, 'Mini Fifties Clock' by The Crafter's Workshop (or similar design)
- Modelling paste (a teaspoon worth)
- White gesso

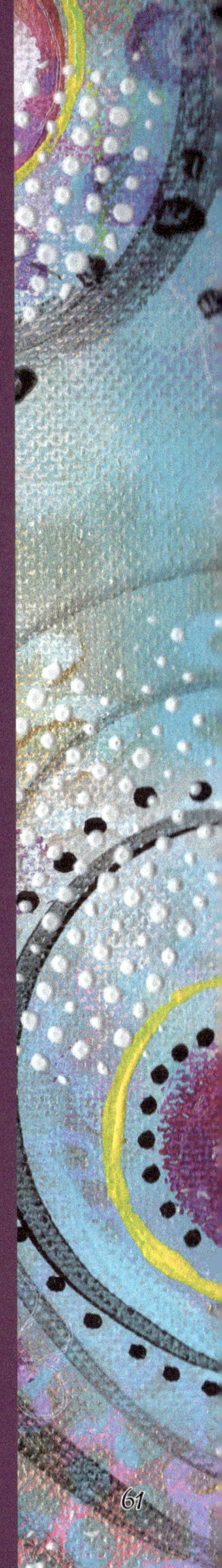

# I'm so excited to show you how to create this painting!

1. Let's start with two delicious colours that ALWAYS go together perfectly: magenta and orange. These colours will create a warm base for our background in an instant! I am thinking of orange and strawberry ice cream...

2. Put a small blob of magenta and white on your palette. You don't actually need much paint at all so always start with a little, and add more if/when needed (it is not that simple to put paint back in a tube!).

3. Dip your fingers (one, two or three of them, just go for it!) in magenta only and spread it on your surface, rubbing in circular motion until there is no paint left on your fingers. Pick up more paint as you go along.

4. Don't fill up the whole surface... Just a few patches here and there. Make sure you don't forget the edges by adding a little paint there too.

5. Now either put an orange blob on your palette or squeeze a little out of the tube onto your finger and spread it on some of the unpainted areas. Go over some of the pink as well (mixing those two colours creates such a fiery orange, wow!).

6. Wipe your hands clean (baby wipes always save the day!) then dip a finger in white paint (just a tiny bit on your fingertip!). White is going to be our tool to blend and soften up our colours. Whipped cream with your ice cream anyone?

7. Start applying the white on an unpainted area and gradually rub it in a circular motion until it mixes with the nearby colours.

8. The more you blend, the softer the colours will look... I find that using three fingers makes it easier to do larger areas! Try to not 'over blend' by concentrating mostly where two colours meet: blending where orange and white meet will give you a soft, light orange transition and blending where magenta and white meet will result in a soft, light pink transition. Awww... So dreamy!!

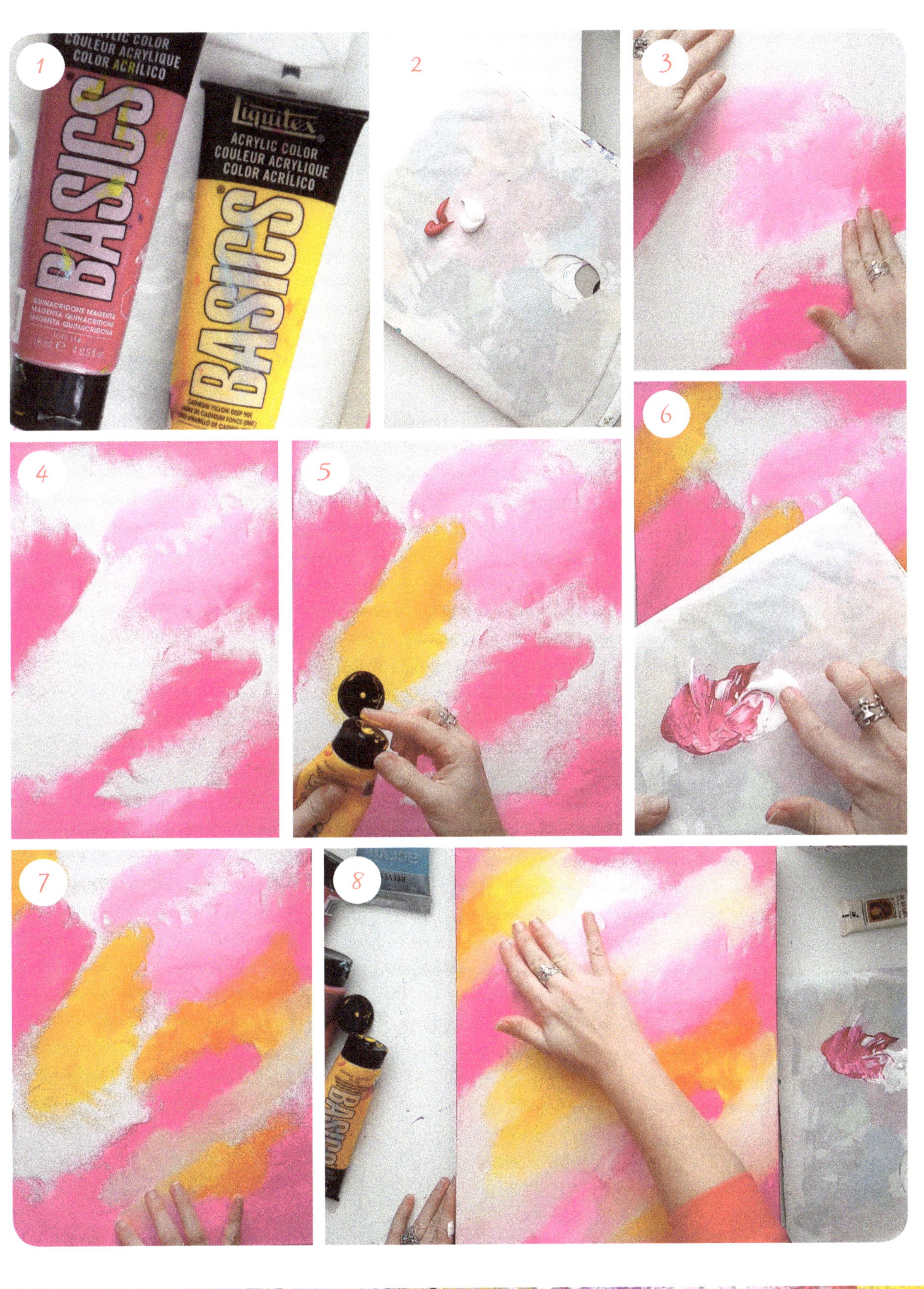

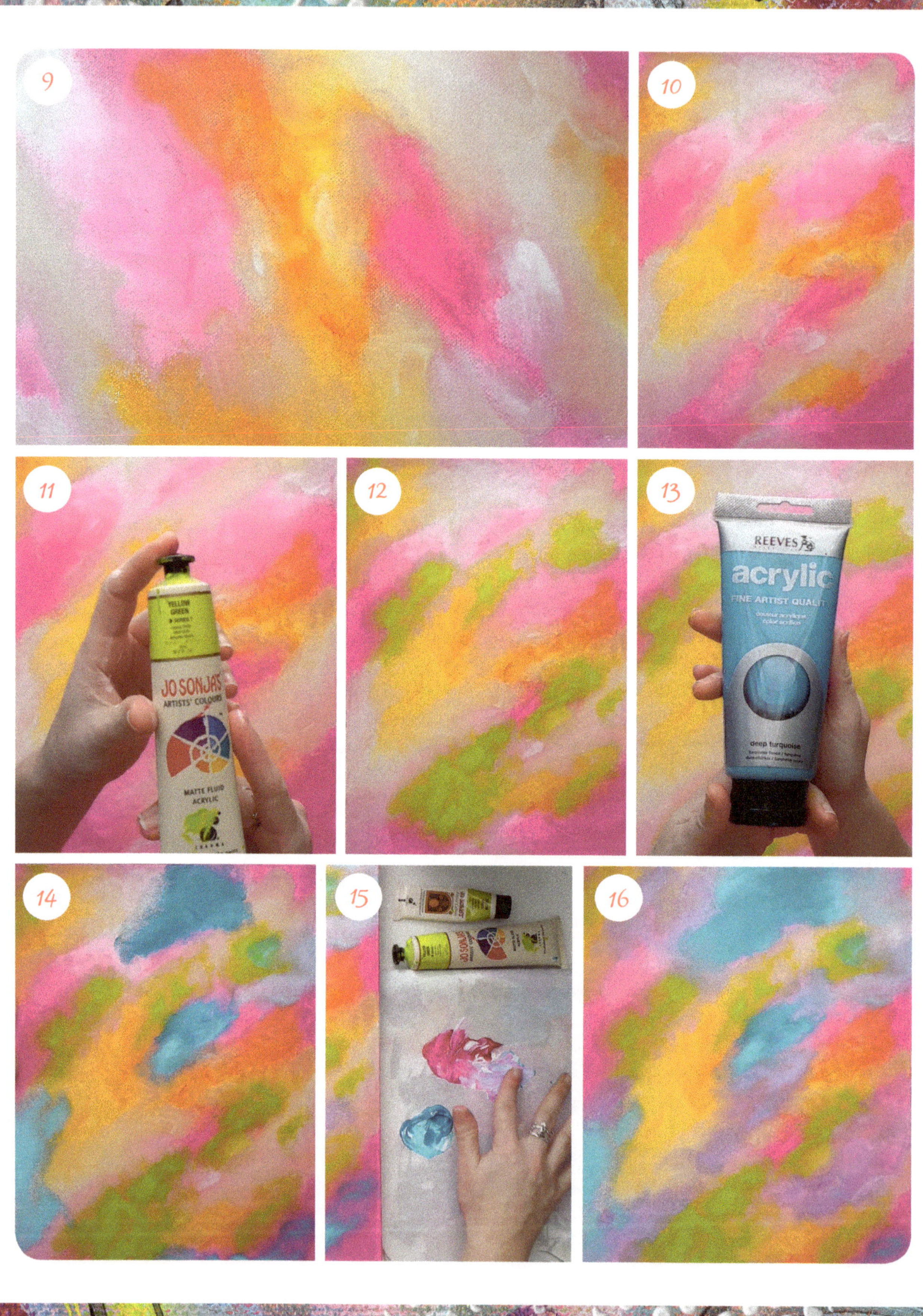
9
10
11
YELLOW
GREEN
JO SONJA'S
ARTISTS' COLOURS
MATTE FLUID
ACRYLIC
12
13
REEVES
acrylic
FINE ARTIST QUALITY
deep turquoise
14
15
JO SONJA'S
16

**9** Up close you may think it looks a little messy and patchy but don't worry, it will be fine in the end! Don't be afraid to leave some of your finger marks as it creates a little texture. Not everything has to be smoothly blended! Keep spreading the paint with your fingers until it looks a little...

**10** ... Like this. Make sure you leave some of the vibrant magenta and orange visible and soften up the rest so you now have various shades of colour and some contrast. When you stand back, everything looks quite 'soft'. Using this simple technique creates stunning backgrounds very quickly and easily but, let's not stop just yet!

**11** A touch of lime green would be perfect to add a little 'oomph'! This 'Yellow Green' by Jo Sonja is one of my favourites because it is very vibrant without being 'fluoro', and also quite opaque straight out of the tube. This is important because a transparent layer of lime green over orange and magenta would not look very nice! Make sure everything is dry before moving on.

As a general rule, if your paint is transparent and you want to make it more opaque, you could mix it with a little gesso or white first. Doing so will indeed increase the opacity but will also lighten up your colour so... If you want your colours to remain true, the trick is to add gesso to your surface FIRST and add the acrylic paint AFTER.
So, if your lime green is transparent, apply some gesso with your finger (in a circular motion like before) where you plan on adding your lime green (soft patches with no harsh lines) and let dry. Don't be scared to add another layer to get a nice opaque surface. Then rub the lime green on top of the dry gesso. This will definitely make your colours pop a lot more!

**12** Once you have added a few patches of lime green, your painting will look a little like this...

**13** Let's now add some turquoise for even more pop! This deep turquoise is quite intense and dark on its own but with a little white, WOW!!

**14** Add a little turquoise here and there, blending some white into it directly on your surface, so you can vary the intensity of the colour.

**15** While everything is still wet on your palette, mix the leftover magenta, deep turquoise and white together to create a light mauve/purple. When possible, you can't go wrong with mixing two colours already used on your surface to create a third complementary colour. Just keep the basics of colour mixing in mind to avoid creating muddy colours!
If you are not sure of the result, then always do a little patch on your palette first.

## " Experimenting is the best way to learn and grow as an artist "

**16** Add a little bit of purple here and there...
Once you are done, your painting may look quite different from mine. Don't worry if your painting does not look exactly like the photos, it is actually a good thing! As an artist you have your own style and touch so feel free to experiment and take a different route at any point if you feel like it! For now, we are focussing on the technique more than the results.

**17** Adding a little white (with paint, ink, pens…) on the final layers (whether you are blending, stencilling, stamping or doodling) is an effective way to add contrast over any vibrant colours! Very lightly dip your fingertip into white paint and…

**18** … Spread the paint here and there, one small area at a time. Now it looks like light clouds are passing through a colourful sunset sky, don't you think? I love this effect!

**19** Time to get either a makeup sponge or a piece of synthetic sponge (different textures will give you slightly different results but anything that looks quite 'dense' will work best).

**20** You can either use the 'Bubble' stencil by Tim Holtz or if you want to try something similar, why not apply a little paint to a piece of bubble wrap then pressing it down on your surface instead? It may not look as neat but it will give you really interesting texture too!

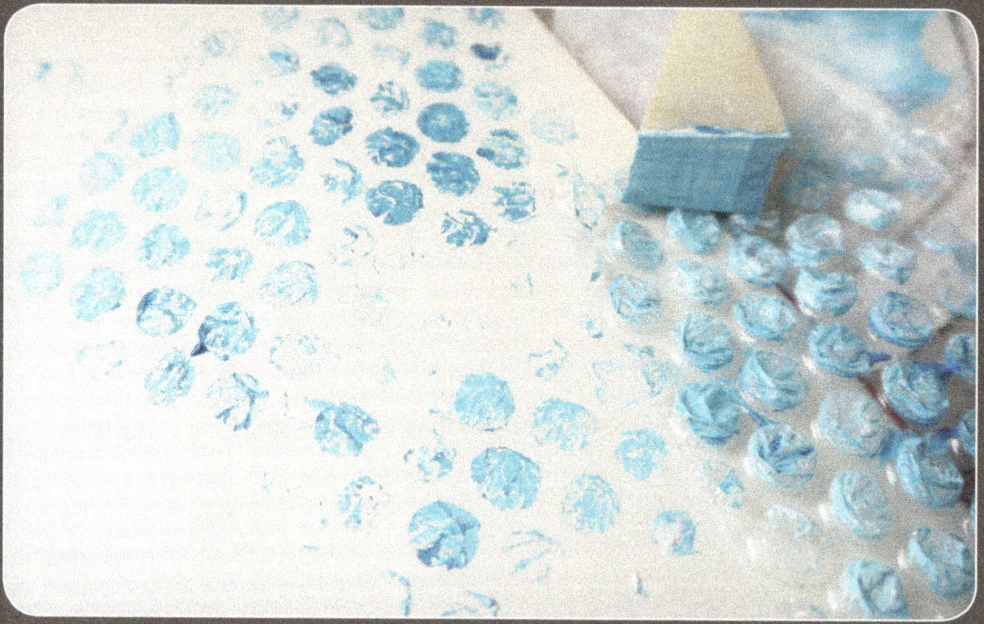

**21** If you are using the stencil, dip your sponge in a mixture of deep turquoise and white (you will get more interesting results if you don't pre-blend the colours here), remove the excess paint on your palette and gently dab the sponge over the stencil, up and down.

**22** Hold the stencil firmly on one end and peel it off a little to check the results. If you want to add more, push it back down and add more paint but avoid covering the whole stencil… Less is more when you want a subtle effect!

**23** This creates playful texture and if you didn't mix your turquoise and white too much, you will also get a funky gradient effect.
Continue stencilling a little in the middle, not forgetting to go near the edges until…

**24** … Your painting looks a little like this (that is: totally gorgeous)!

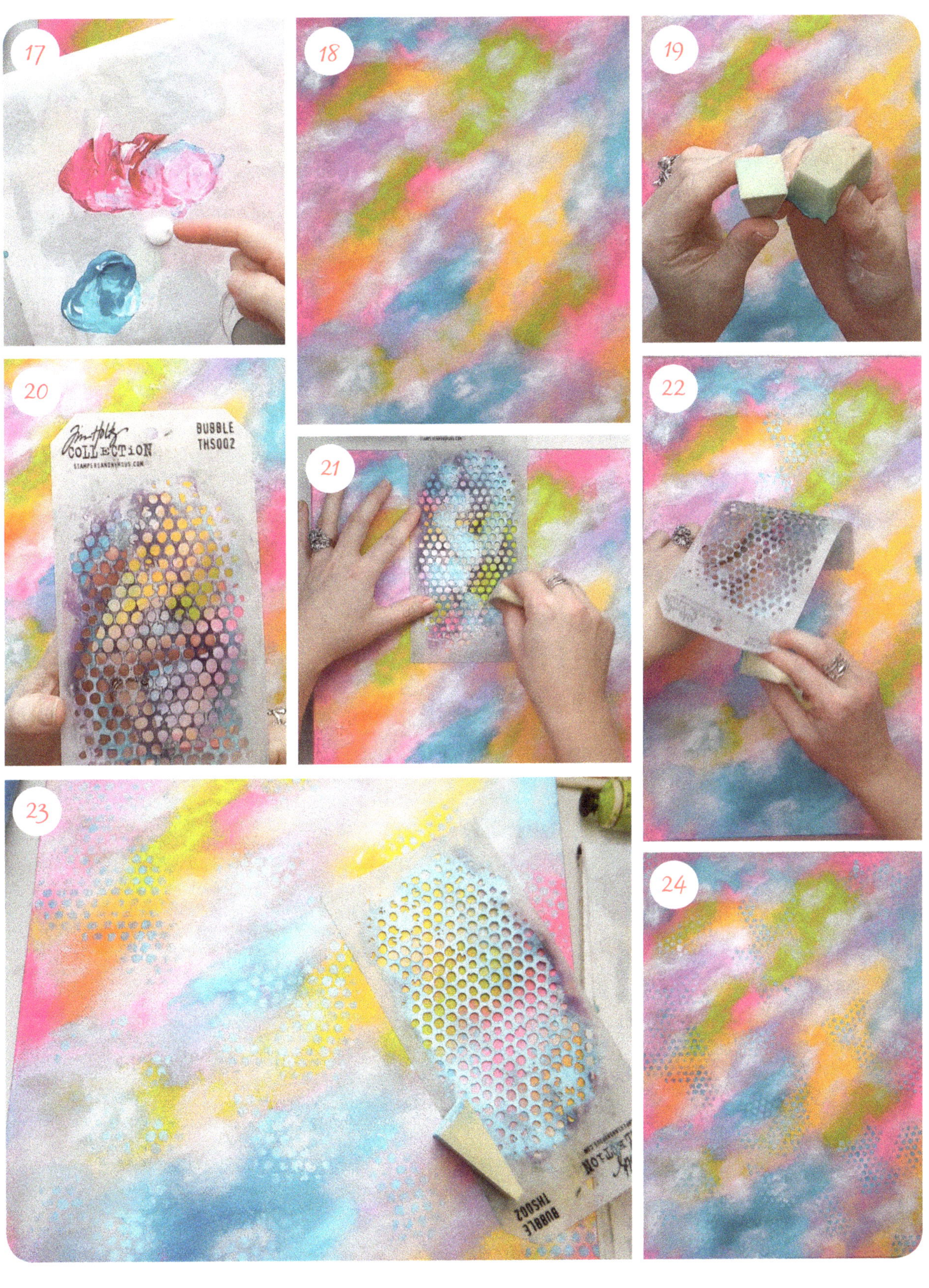

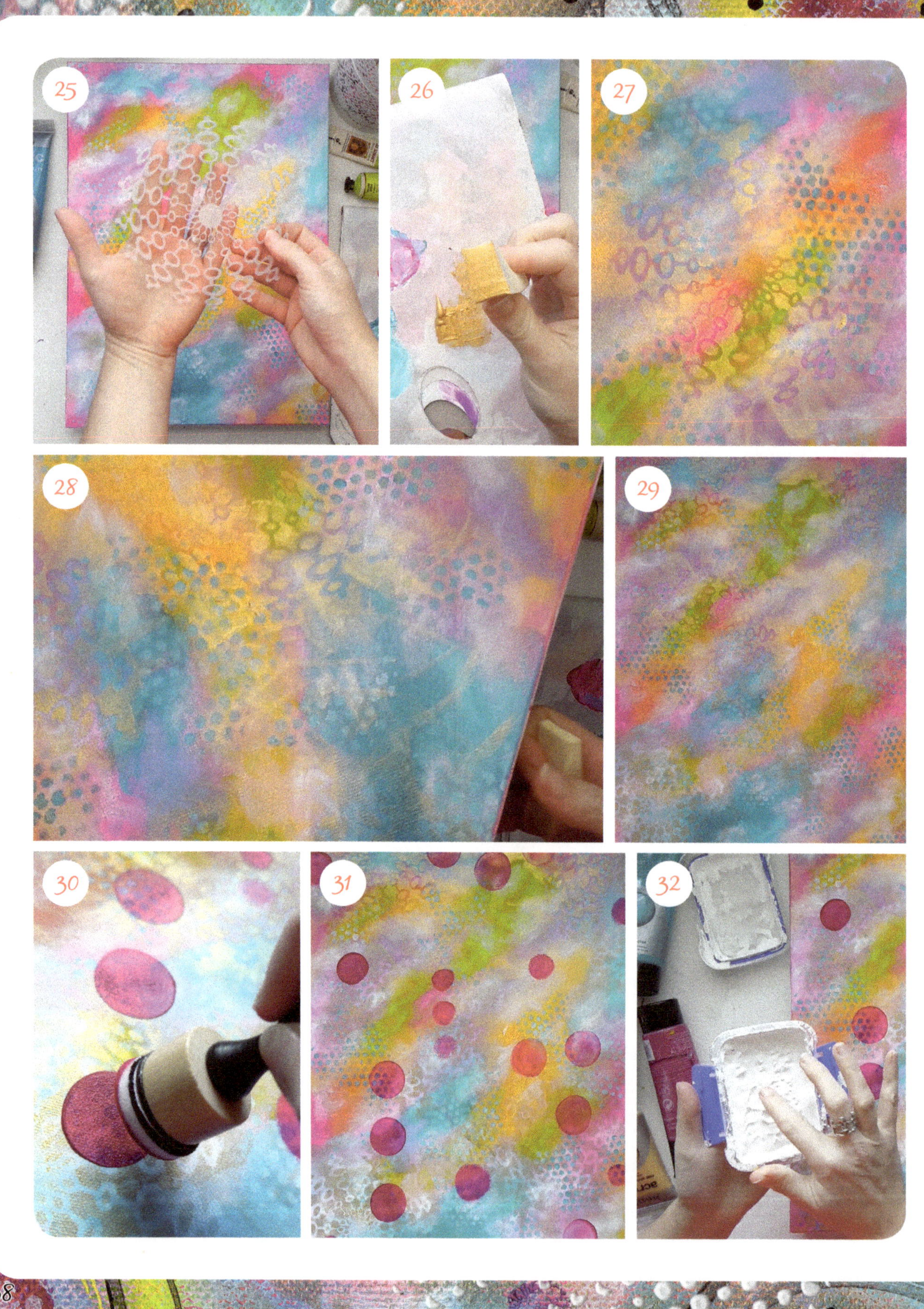

# How to add subtle background texture...

**25** The way to add subtle background texture here is to use a stencil with a delicate/ornate design and a colour that will not stand out much. Metallic paint such as gold works well for this because it brings subtle colour while leaving the layers underneath visible when looking at the painting from the front. It also gives us shimmer when looking at the painting from the side or when the light reflects directly on it, creating different moods... If you don't want to use gold, you could use one of the background colours with a little white as you stencil.

Here I am using the 'Mini Fifties Clock' stencil/mask by The Crafter's Workshop. I don't expect you to run to the shops to get it so use anything with an interesting pattern. This one is quite delicate because the 'arms' are very thin and just held up by a circle in the center, so be very careful not to move the stencil too much while painting over it.

*"A stencil has shapes cut out to allow you to create a positive image whereas a mask is a 'cover' allowing you to create a negative image"*

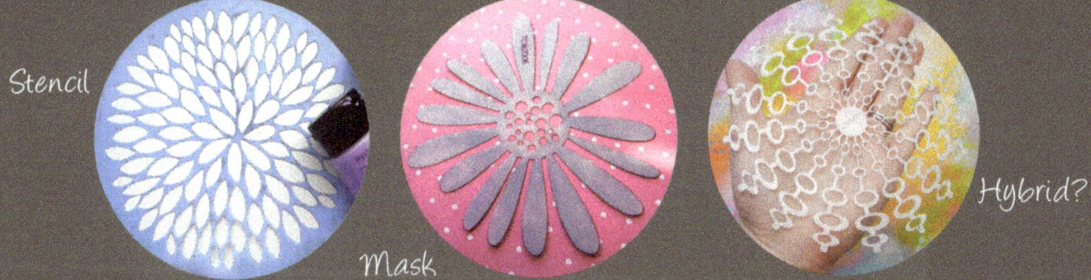


**26** Dip your sponge in gold paint, remove the excess and dab very gently, up and down.

**27** Remove the stencil and admire the awesome results! Stencil a few more patterns around your surface, as well as partly over the edges for more interest.

**28** Dip the sponge in gold again but this time, dab it straight onto your surface, here and there (without the stencil) to create subtle lines and marks. Your painting will feel more unified now that you have a little gold on most of your surface.

**29** The effect is subtle when the painting is not in direct light but that is exactly what we wanted.

**30** Now let's add more obvious marks for contrast: use the same magenta paint as before to create circles. You could either use a small round blending tool like this one by Tim Holtz, or simply dip your finger in paint and rub the surface to create a circle. Easy!

**31** Vary the size of the circles: add single ones, some in a line and some over the edges.

**32** Now pick up the smallest amount possible of gesso (or white paint) with your finger.

**33** Carefully place your finger in the center of a magenta circle and rub in a circular motion to create a smaller circle. Repeat for all of them, don't be too neat!

## Still going around in circles!

**34** Ready for more?
Let's 'echo' the circles you just painted, but with outlines instead of 'full' circles.
Grab an empty roll of toilet paper (or similar) and add a good blob of yellow paint on your palette in a rough circular shape, just a little wider than the roll. Dip the roll in the paint and turn it around a few times on the spot so it collects paint on the rim.

**35** Press the roll on top of some (or all if you are in the mood!) the existing circles (big and small). This adds a subtle thin border and therefore, extra interest. Let this dry for a while - the paint is a little thicker than before so it will take a little longer. Patience my friend!
I will admit it was not a virtue I was born with... Or have acquired yet!

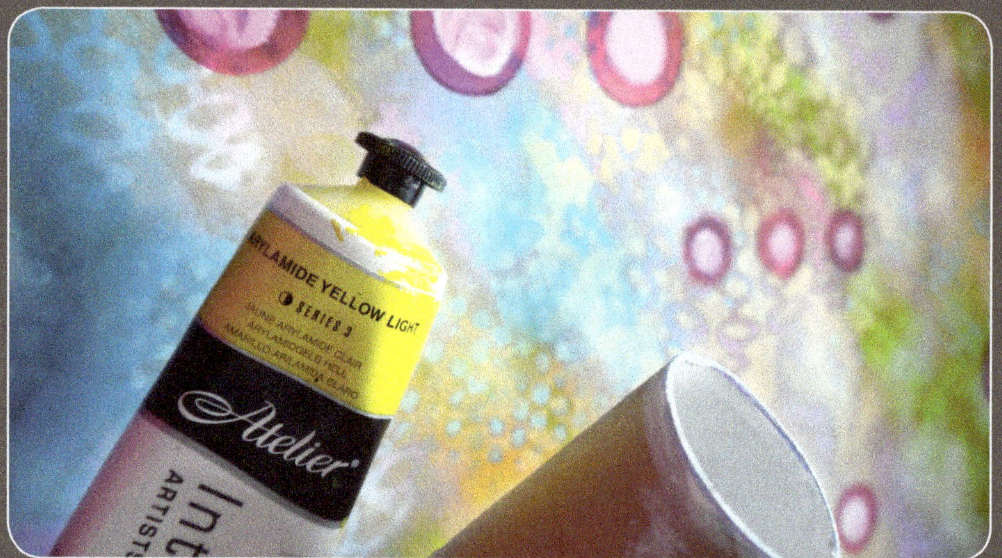

**36** Now dip your finger in the leftover yellow paint and rub it around some of the circles. Go half way around some of them and all the way around on others. Remember, variation is key!

**37** Repeat with a little turquoise (mixed with white to lighten it up). Clean your finger with a baby wipe and repeat with white paint.

**38** Now dip your finger in dark purple paint and create little dots by dabbing it on your surface. Just dip then dab until your finger feels dry, and repeat. Follow some of the curves here and there until you have a few marks around the whole area of your surface.

**39** Your painting will be similar to mine but of course, not identical (thankfully!).

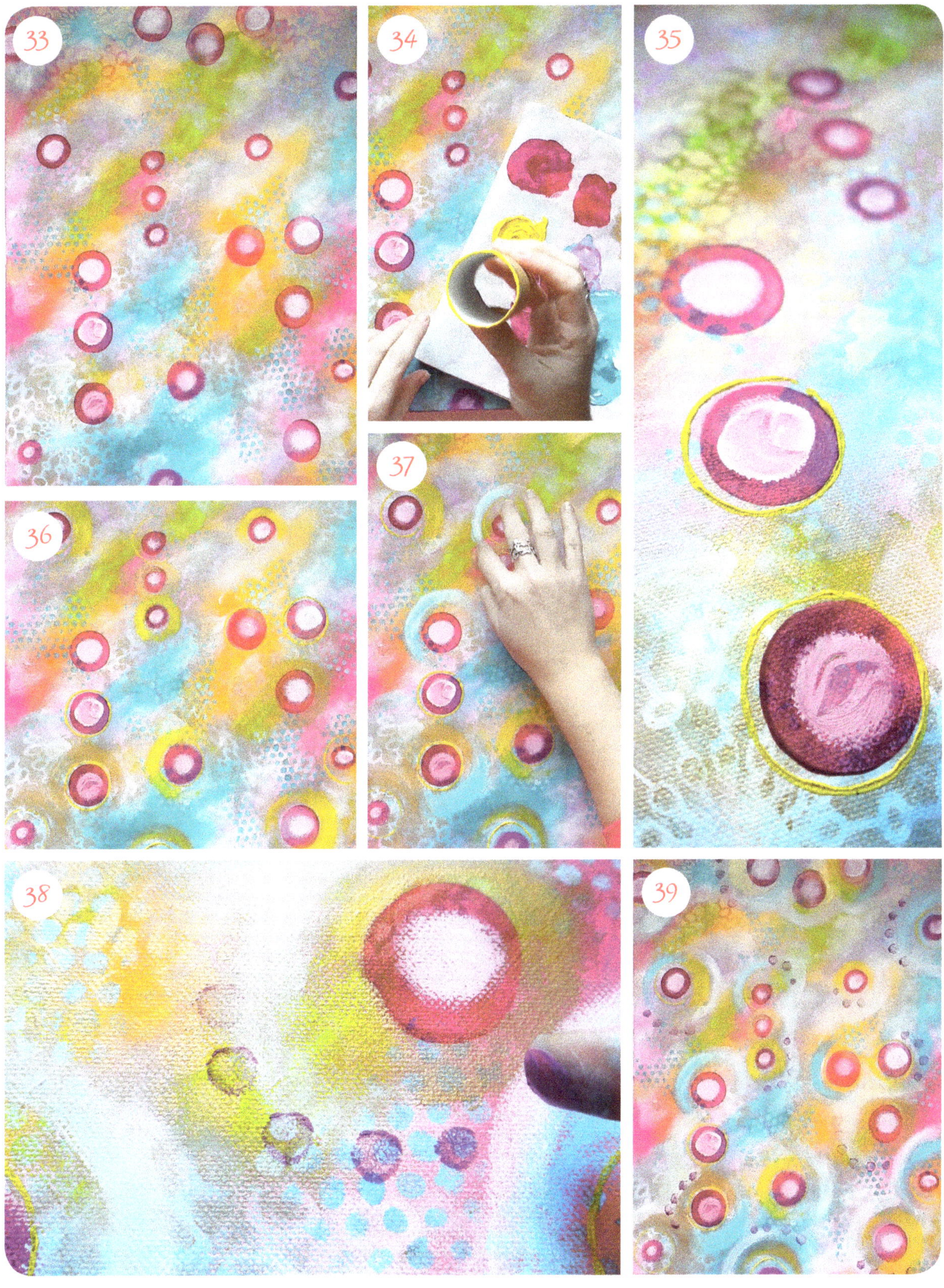

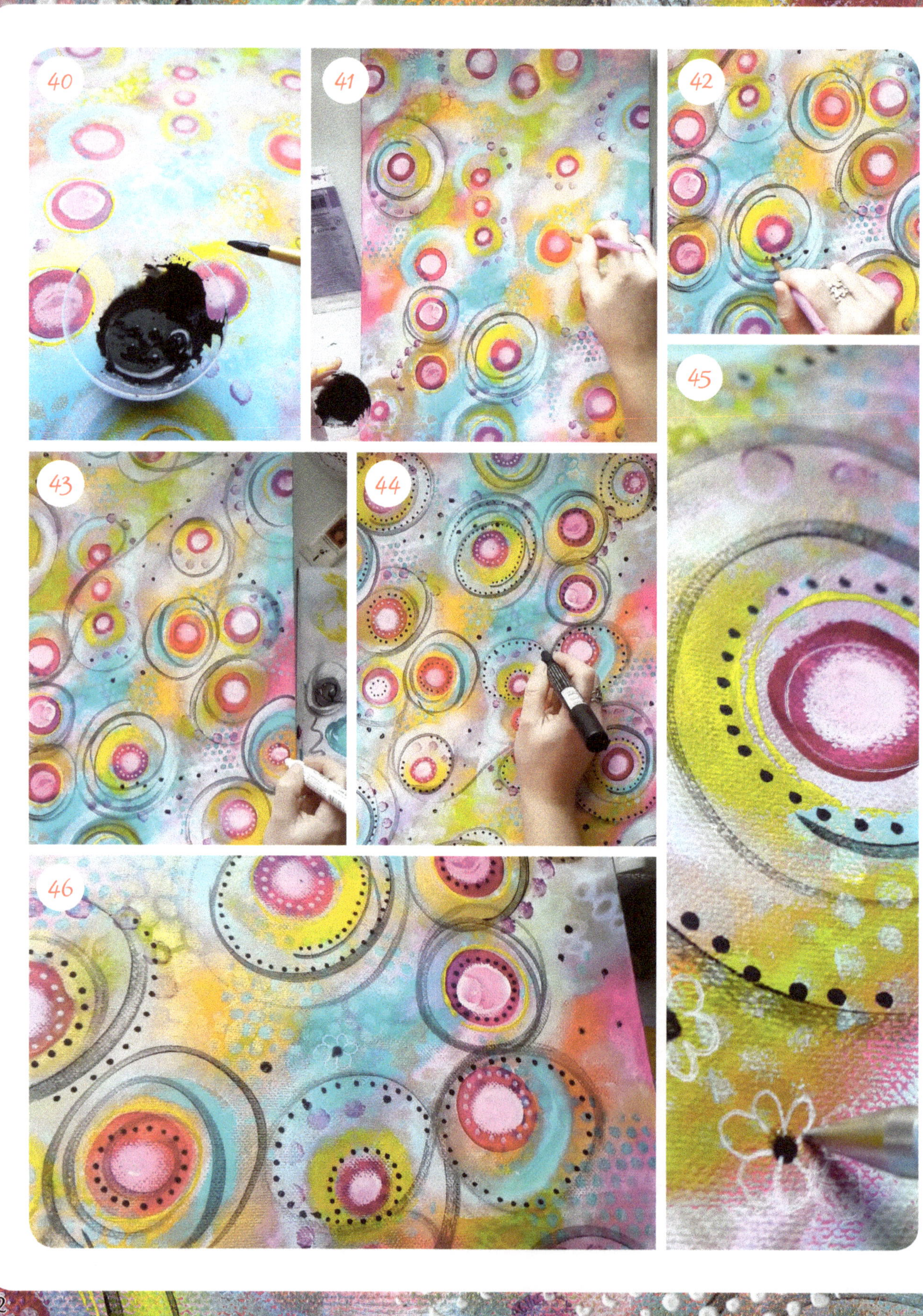

# The all important details...

Now that you have a gorgeous background with lots of texture and beautiful colours blending together, you need to add some details on the foreground for a little pop. Black and white are always perfect for this!

**40** Dilute some black acrylic paint with a little water in a small container (not too much water so the pigments don't separate). You can also use black fluid acrylic paint (my favourite one is the 'FW Liquid Acrylic' by Daler Rowney), India ink or drawing ink (I like the 'Waterproof Drawing Ink' in Carbon Black by Atelier). These options are easier and a lot more fluid than most acrylic paints but since we only need so little here, they are not worth buying unless you plan on using them again later.

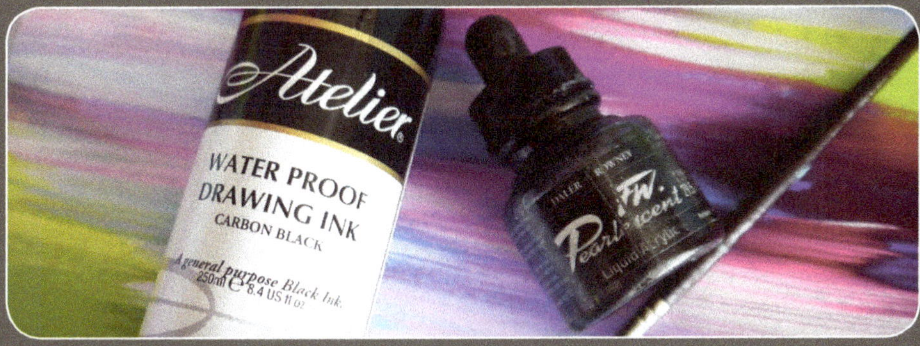

**41** Dip a fine tip brush in the diluted paint and hold it loosely to allow for fluid movement. Lightly trace circles and spirals around your painted circles. Some lines can overlap, or join... Just go with the flow, but don't press too hard.

**42** Now what could be more perfect to compliment our circles than lots of tiny circles/dots? Gold would be great since we put gold paint on our background but it wouldn't stand out as much as black and white so, let's stick to those two colours.
First, add a few random dots here and there using your brush dipped in black paint...
And let everything dry.

**43** Then, grab a white marker pen (such as a medium tip Sharpie or Posca) and add little dots wherever they would bring good contrast, such as over the darker colours (magenta and turquoise). Feel free to add some on top of the light colours too! Let dry.

**44** Now use a black marker pen (such as a 1.8mm black Posca) and add a few dots, this time following some of the curves you hand painted, and anywhere you like.

**45** Finally, add some 'secret' details (the kind you don't usually notice until you study the painting a little closely) using a white fine tip gel paint (I like the 1mm Pentel White Hybrid Gel pen) and draw little doodles... Add petals around some of the hand painted black dots to create tiny flowers for example.

**46** The result is really energizing and interesting... And gives the viewer so much to look at!

# How to fix something that is bugging you...

**47** Don't like something on your painting? Take action AS SOON AS you notice! If you ignore it, I guarantee all you will see at the end is 'that bit you don't like', and by then it may not be possible to fix it!

For example, all the black lines on my canvas are quite round and curvy except for one that is a little straight... I can be picky, I know, but thankfully, it isn't too late to change it!
I use gesso with my finger over the line I want to disappear, and a little around it too.
I let it dry then apply more gesso until the line is barely noticeable...
Now I have a blank area on which I can repeat some of the steps we have taken so far:
- First I blend some of the colours we used in the background (lime green and light turquoise)
- I let everything dry, rub in a little gold, let that dry again then...
- I add a few details (some hand painted black dots) and I am ready to keep going!

**48** You really wouldn't know that annoying black line was ever there so now I can add a thin black curvy line instead. Depending on the change you want to make, you may need to adapt the colours, add another pink circle or little dots with your black and white pens.

# Modelling paste for the final touches

For our final layer to stand out, we need an element that is:
- In a contrasting colour that still complements our colour scheme (such as white)
- In keeping with our dots/circle theme
- Much smaller than any of the circles created previously
The random pattern of tiny circles in Tim Holtz's 'Dot Fade' stencil will be perfect for this with modelling paste (it is already white and as an added bonus, will add texture you can feel).

**49** First, add a blob of modelling paste to your palette and pick it up with the back of a palette knife (of any size) just like you would pick up butter to spread on your toast... You could use an old credit/store card instead of a palette knife.

**50** Hold your stencil firmly with one hand so you have good contact with your surface and spread the paste over it. Preferably one stroke, in one direction only.

**51** Cover part of the stencil to get little patches of dots, not the entire stencil. Carefully peel it away without smudging your paste.

**52** Isn't that just beautiful?? I love the various sizes of dots we get with no work at all!

**53** Clean the back of the stencil with a dry cloth/tissue in case some paste seeped through...

**54** ... And repeat the process of applying paste, gently peeling off and cleaning the back of the stencil in a few areas and... Voilà! A taste of summer all year round :-)

*The finished painting is showcased on page 104*

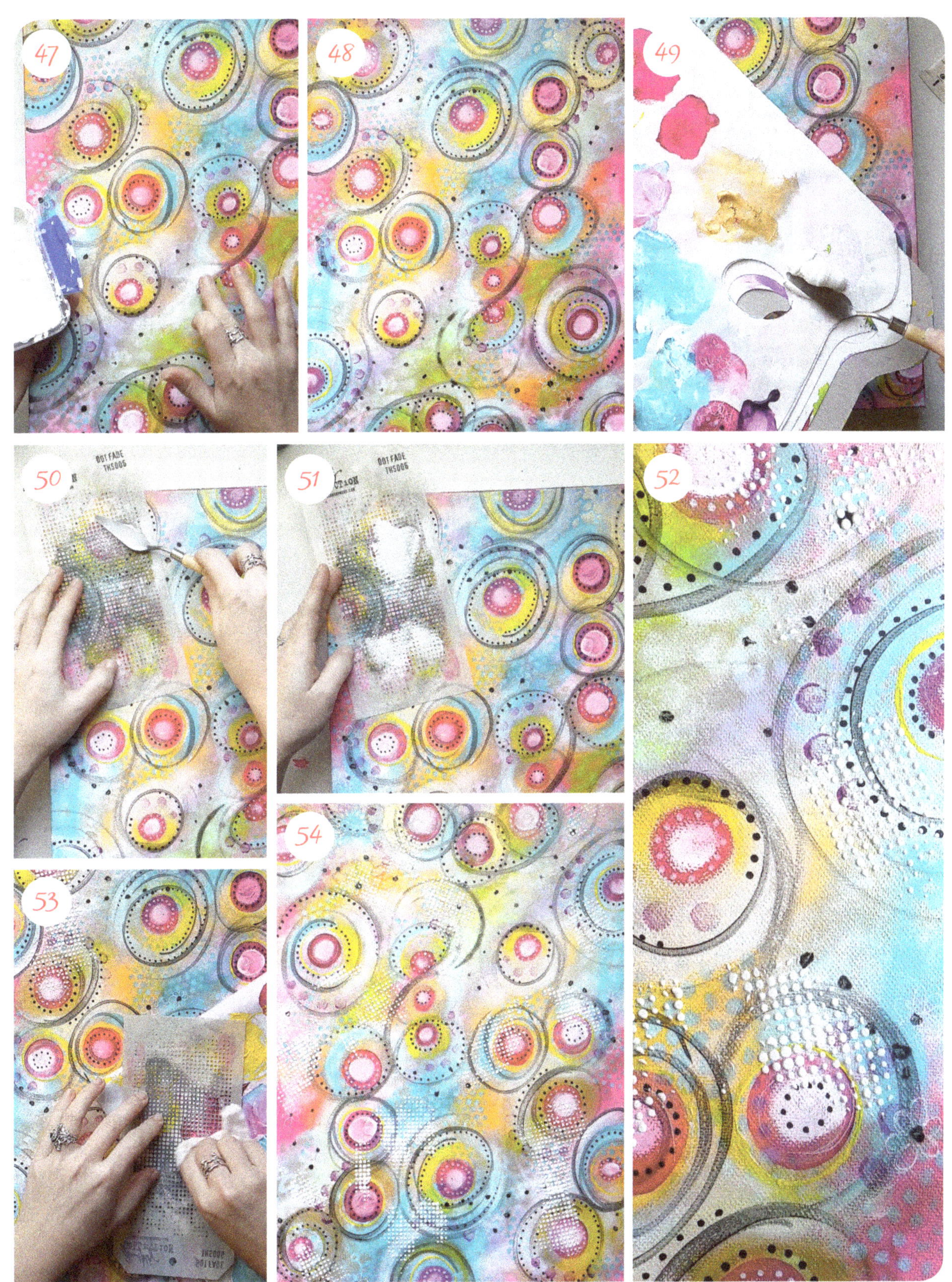

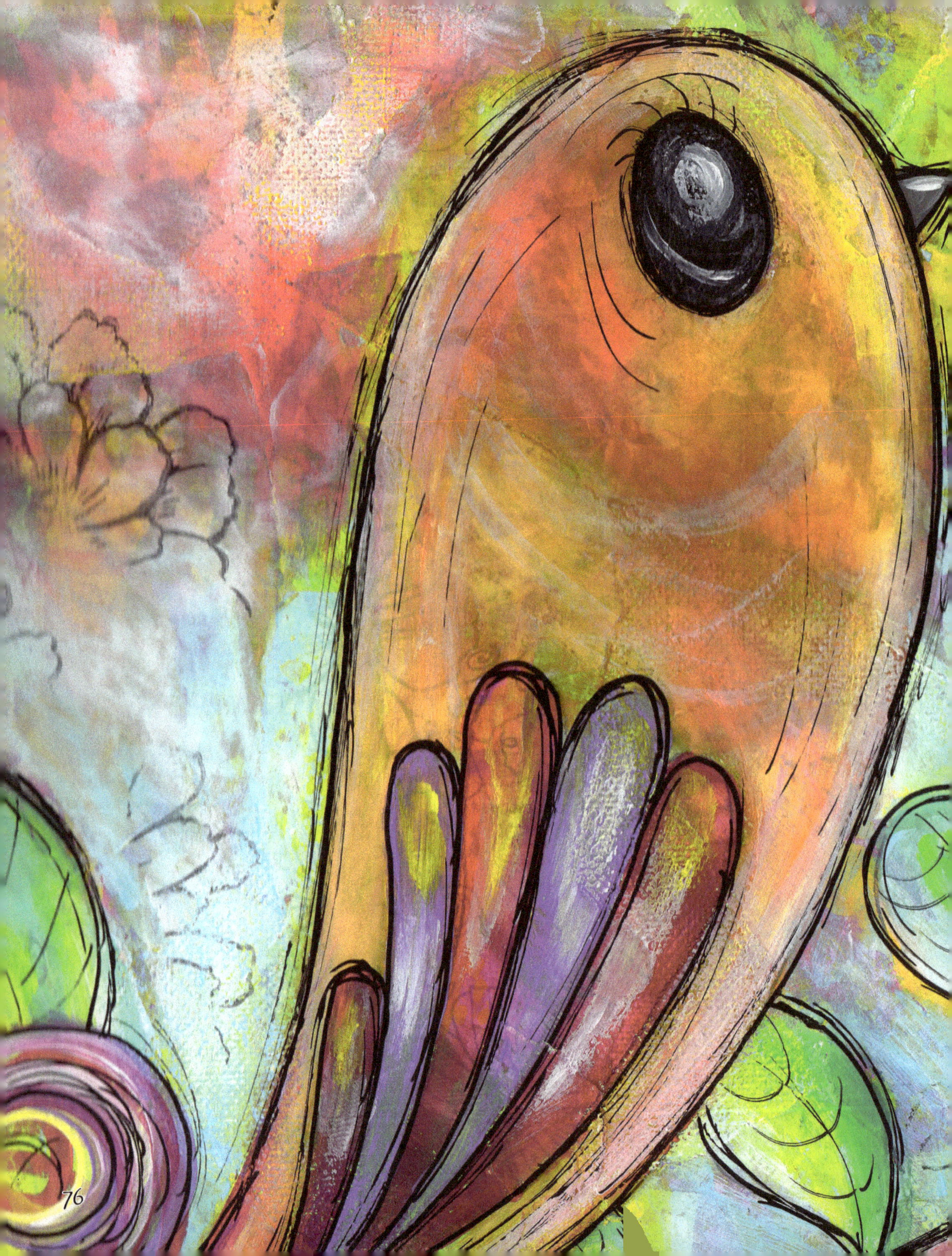

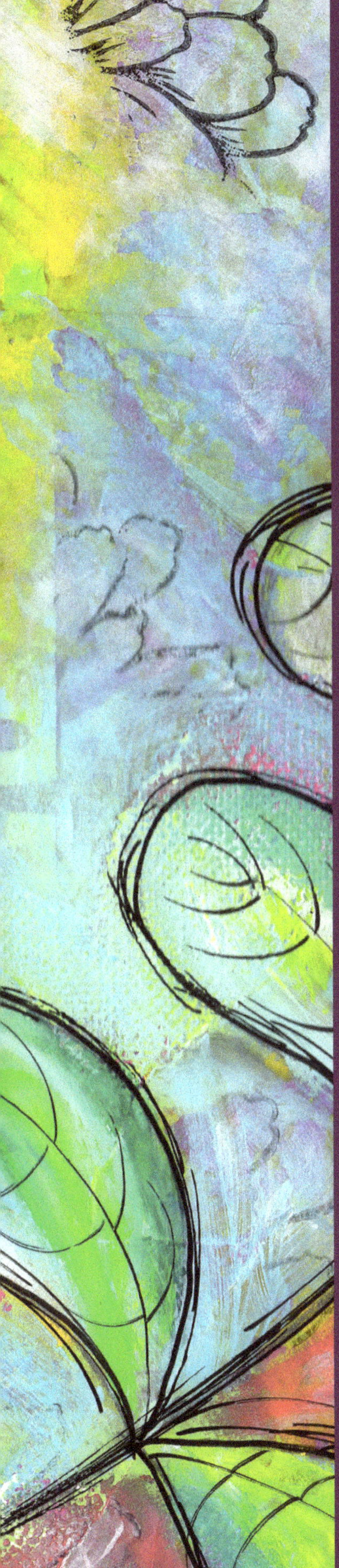
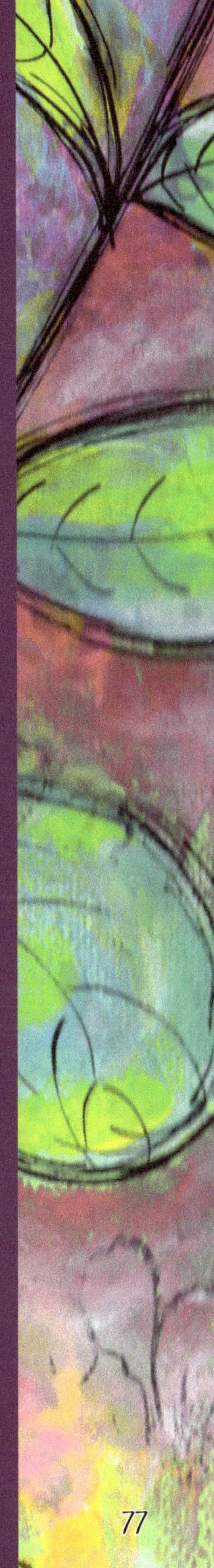



# We all need
## a little
# Whimsy

### Get in touch
### with your soft side!

Birds are so fragile and innocent, aren't they?
But whimsical birds? Ahhhh... Well...
They just turn your heart into a marshmallow!

Follow me along on this fun journey to creating
the sweetest little bird you have ever seen!

I will show you how to make a lovely textured
background using collaged paper and how to
add paint on top for interest.

You will also learn how to incorporate a main focal
point into your painting and how to bring all the
elements together to make your painting feel whole.

Make sure you keep this birdie close by as a reminder
of how fragile and precious we all are... I am sure he
will be singing lovely songs to you if you let him!

### Recommended supplies

- A few pieces of thin scrapbooking paper
  (or giftwrap/magazine pages)
- Acrylic paint: light blue/turquoise, magenta,
  yellow, medium green, Phtalo/Viridian green,
  light and dark orange, mauve, rose pink, black,
  white (or gesso)
- Plastic card (old credit/library/store/gift card)
- Fine tip black marker
- Stamp of your choice (flower, words, etc)
- 'Stone Gray' Stazon inkpad
- Gel medium

# Collage? Yes, please!

I don't know about you but, I have a hard time preventing myself from buying pretty sheets of paper... There are so many gorgeous designs, it really is an addiction! I admit I don't always know what I will do with them (other than just look at them and smile)! Thankfully I discovered paper can be the perfect tool to add texture and dimension to a background! So rejoice because now we have a completely justified reason to buy pretty papers: we 'need' them for our art! You are welcome :)

**1** I recommend you get a scrapbooking paper pad that will last you for many, many projects. Pads have a good selection of designs and colours, and are more economical than buying paper by the sheet. Thin paper works better than cardstock for this. You could also use wrapping paper or magazine pages for very interesting effects... It is called 'recycling'!

Select a few sheets you like with a few different patterns and colours. The paper will be used in the background only and will be covered up with paint later so no need to use anything expensive or that you are really attached to.

**2** Tear various uneven shapes out of the paper (you can tear pieces off the pad without pulling the sheets out), making sure the edges look a little torn to create some texture.

**3** If some pieces have straight edges then gently tear them away.

**4** Now this may feel strange for any 'I want it all to be neat and perfect' people out there! You are probably looking at your bits of paper thinking that Mimi has lost the plot... True, I did, a long time ago! But trust me, the reason why the edges must be ripped is to avoid any harsh lines when you layer the pieces of paper on your surface.

## How to safely glue paper to your surface...

**5** Gel medium is my close friend whenever I want to incorporate paper into my art because it glues and seals the paper well - whether it is in an art journal, on acrylic paper or canvas. My favourite one is by Faber Castell but unfortunately, it only comes in a tiny jar that doesn't last long! So I also use the Matte Gel Medium by Liquitex but other brands are fine too.

**6** Either pour some gel medium into a little cup or use it straight from the jar... Dip your square wash brush in the gel and spread a generous amount on your surface a bit bigger than the first piece of paper you want to use. Press the paper into the gel. Dip your brush in your cup/jar and spread another generous layer on top of the paper. Go back and forth and up and down to ensure the paper and edges are completely covered.

**7** The next piece of paper will slightly overlap the previous one. Again, spread the gel, apply the paper, hold it down with one finger if you need while you spread more gel all over it.

**8** Repeat this process, making sure you pay special attention to the edges as we don't want these peeling off later on!

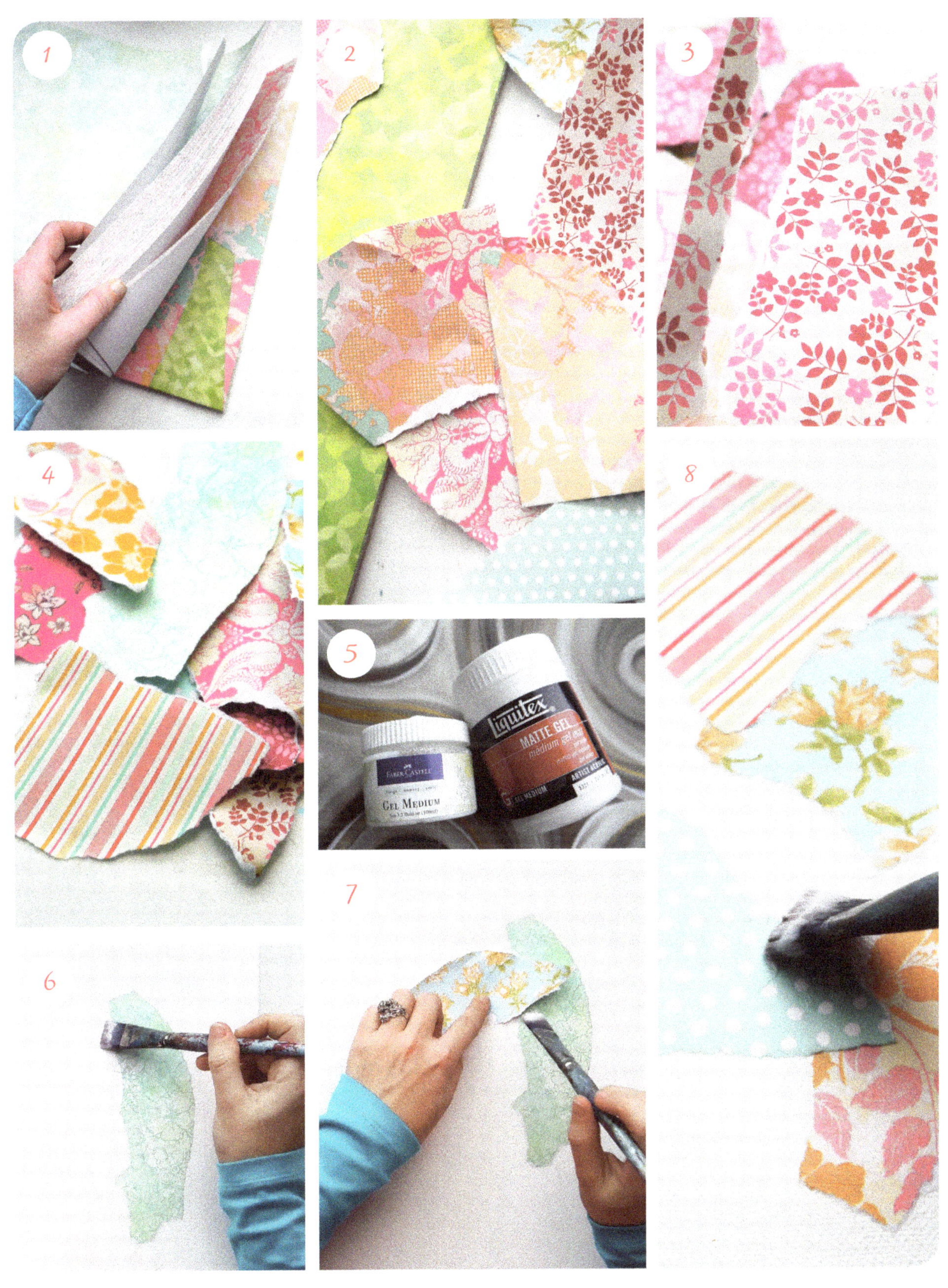
FABER-CASTELL
Gel Medium
Liquitex
MATTE GEL
medium gel mat

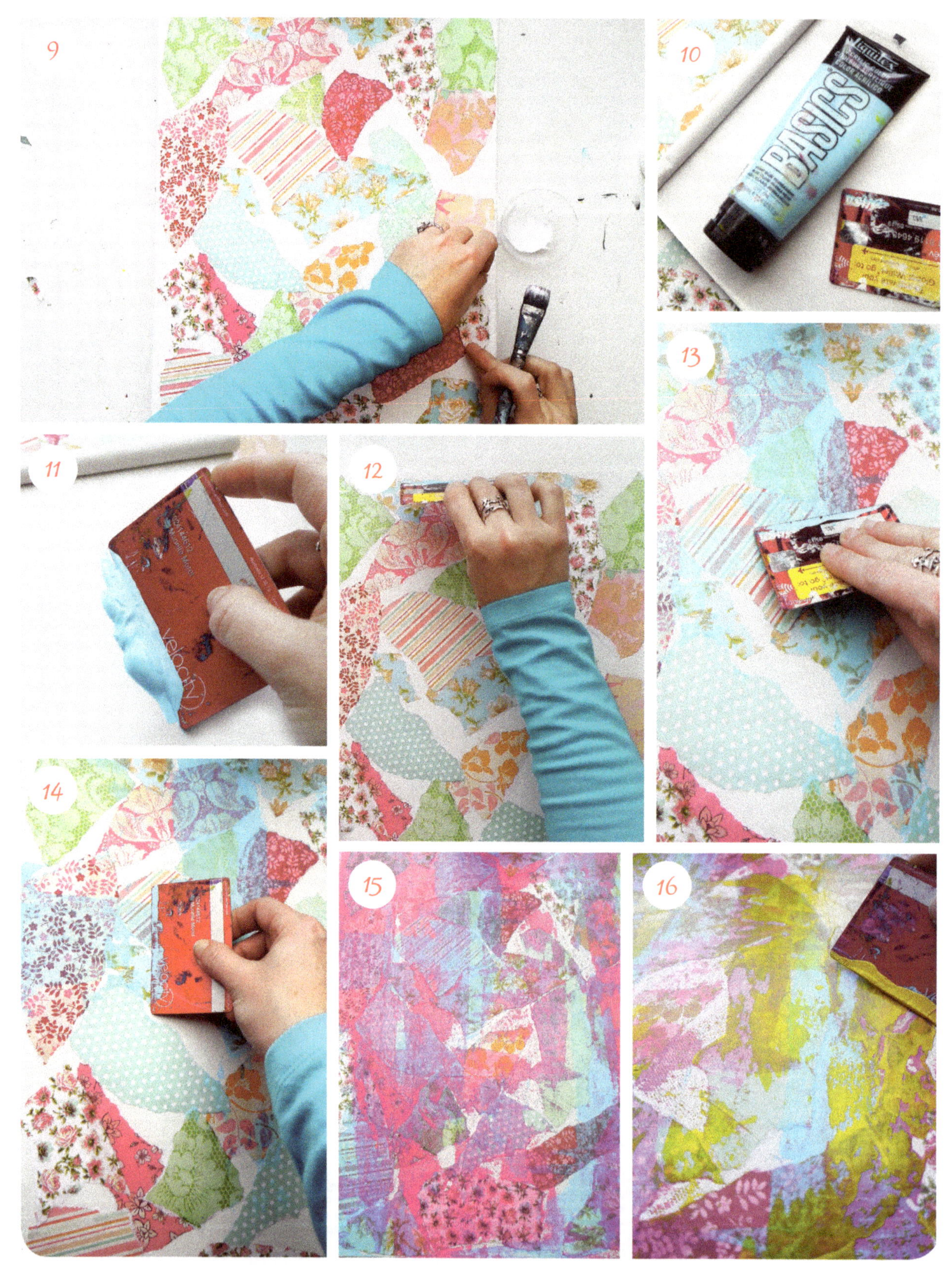

**9** Cover most of your surface but not entirely. Here I left a few gaps on purpose to allow the texture of the canvas to show through and contrast with the smoothness of the paper. Once you are done with your collage and everything is dry, inspect your collage up close. If you find any edges lifting up then add a little gel medium to your fingertip or brush, spread it under the 'culprit', press it down and add more medium on top. Let dry.

## Painting with a plastic card

**10** For this step you will need some light turquoise acrylic paint, your palette and a plastic card. An old credit/library/store/gift card will do the trick (I am glad to have finally found some use for my Velocity card!!).

**11** Spread some paint on your palette in a rough line, about the length of your card. Dip the long edge of your card in the paint and move it up and down to pick up a little paint on both sides.

**12** Line up your paint-covered card with the top edge of your surface...

**13** ... And drag it in a vertical motion until no paint is left. Just keep the edge of the card in contact with your surface the whole time.

**14** Now flip the card around to use the paint on the other side and line it up with the left edge of your surface. Drag it in a horizontal motion until no paint is left.

**15** Pick up more paint as you go along, and drag your card a few more times from the bottom and right edge of your surface. Then, while the blue paint is still wet, repeat the process with magenta so the two colours mix here and there to create a lovely purple.

**16** If you add yellow while the other colours are wet, you will create mud so let everything dry first so your yellow stays just that: yellow! Pick up some paint and drag your card, this time staying away from the edges. If you don't press too hard, your card will glide over the edges of the paper and create funky patterns... How cool is that? Have fun with it and experiment by going up and down then left to right, using both sides of the card. Let dry.

If you have any leftover paint on your palette, don't throw it away! Grab your art journal (or another canvas or sheet of acrylic paper) and use your card to spread it, just like you did earlier.
This will not only avoid wasting precious paint but also give you an awesome pre-painted background! A little bit of paint is often enough to fill several pages in an art journal. Perfect!

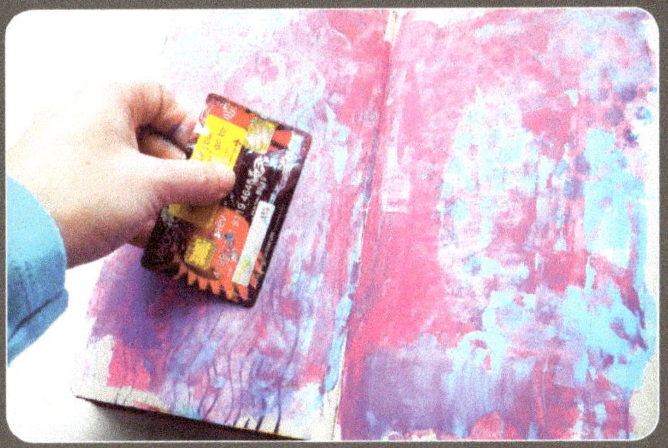

**17** Let's introduce a contrasting green on our background. I love the vibrancy of this colour but it is a little too strong in comparison with the other ones we just used! Let's tone it down with some white until we have a delicious 'apple green'... You can simply mix the two colours together with your finger as we won't need much.

**18** Start with spreading the paint with one finger (or two to go faster) on one of the edges of your surface, then over some of the nearby colours (at this stage you don't need to worry about the collaged paper anymore). You won't create mud as long as everything is dry!

**19** Add some green on any previously unpainted areas (where your canvas or paper is still showing through), as well as on some of the edges of your surface. Make sure your little green patches don't have any harsh edges then let everything dry.

## Look who just arrived!

**20** A big sweet bird is going to be the star of the show! If you are not comfortable with drawing one from scratch, that's OK because I drew a simple one for you. You can download the template, right here: **mimibondi.com/art/free-whimsical-bird-template** I included a large bird (great for canvasses) and a small one suitable for art journalling (or as a companion to the big one!). Print it (preferably on cardstock) and cut it out.

**21** Now decide where your bird should go so the composition feels balanced. If you are unsure, I suggest dividing your surface into 4 parts (an imaginary vertical line in the middle and a horizontal one in the middle too). Place your template where the lines would meet. Leaving your bird right in the center would feel unnatural so move him a bit to the right of your vertical line and a bit below your horizontal line. Perfect spot!

**22** Now use your template as a guide and trace around his body with a pencil.

## Let's add some greenery...

**23** Your bird will need a branch to stand on! Draw a simple curve coming from the right edge (under the tail) to the left edge of your surface (almost to the top but not quite).

**24** Now draw simple curvy leaves on either side of the branch. Try varying the size of each one a little to create more interest.

Refer to the image on the right where I emphasized my lines so you can see what I did. Feel free to adapt the size and shape to your style!

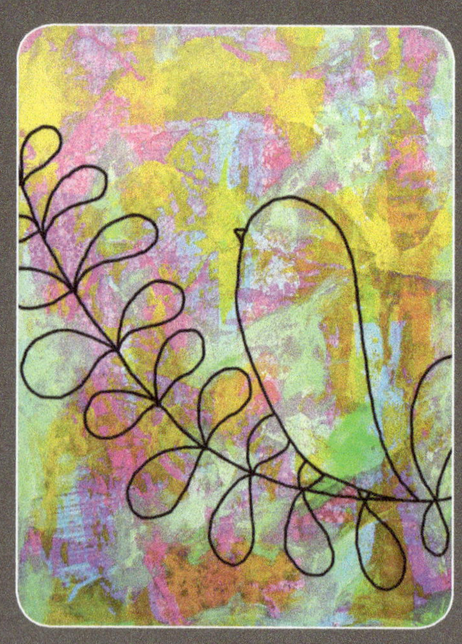

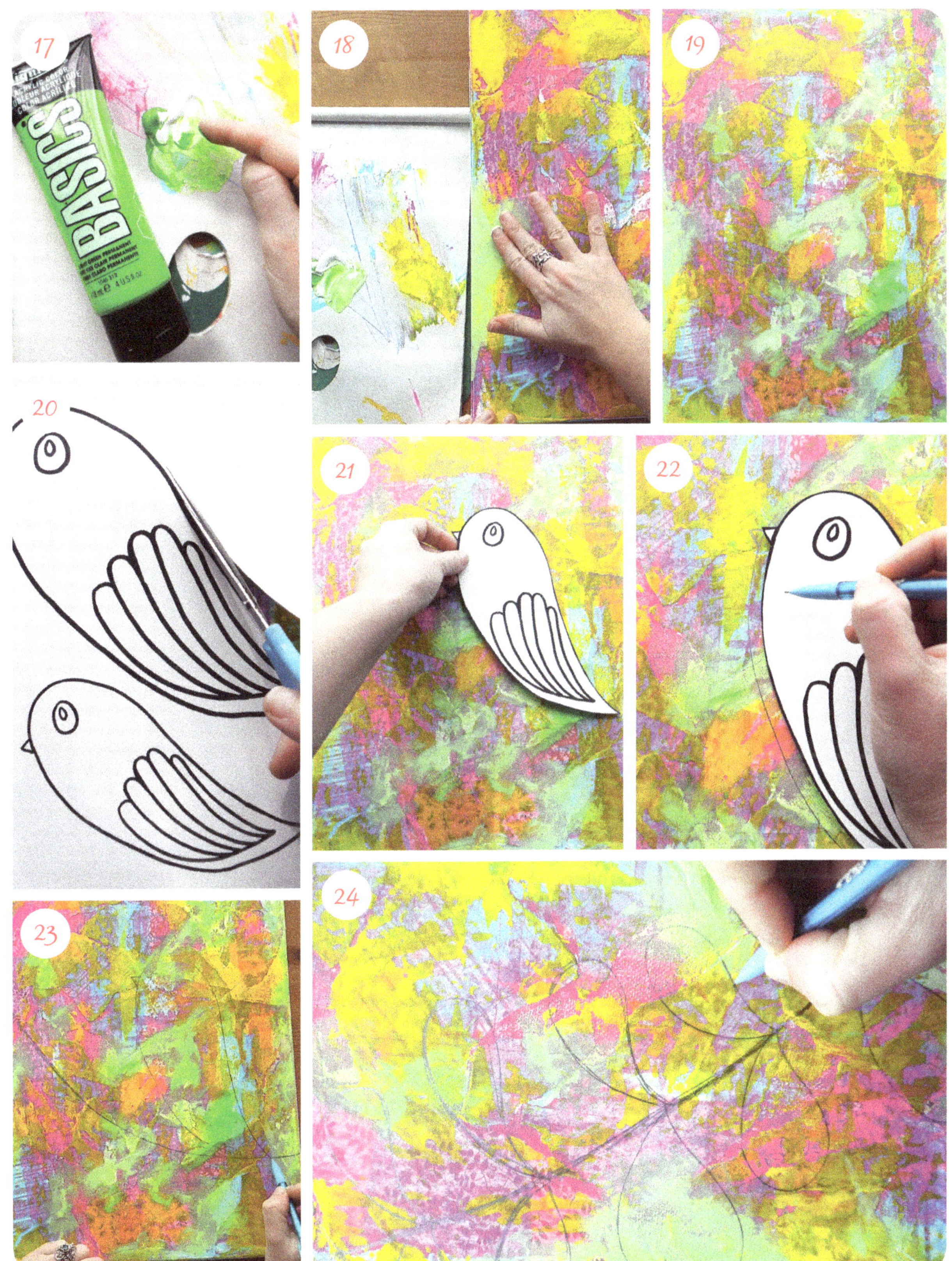

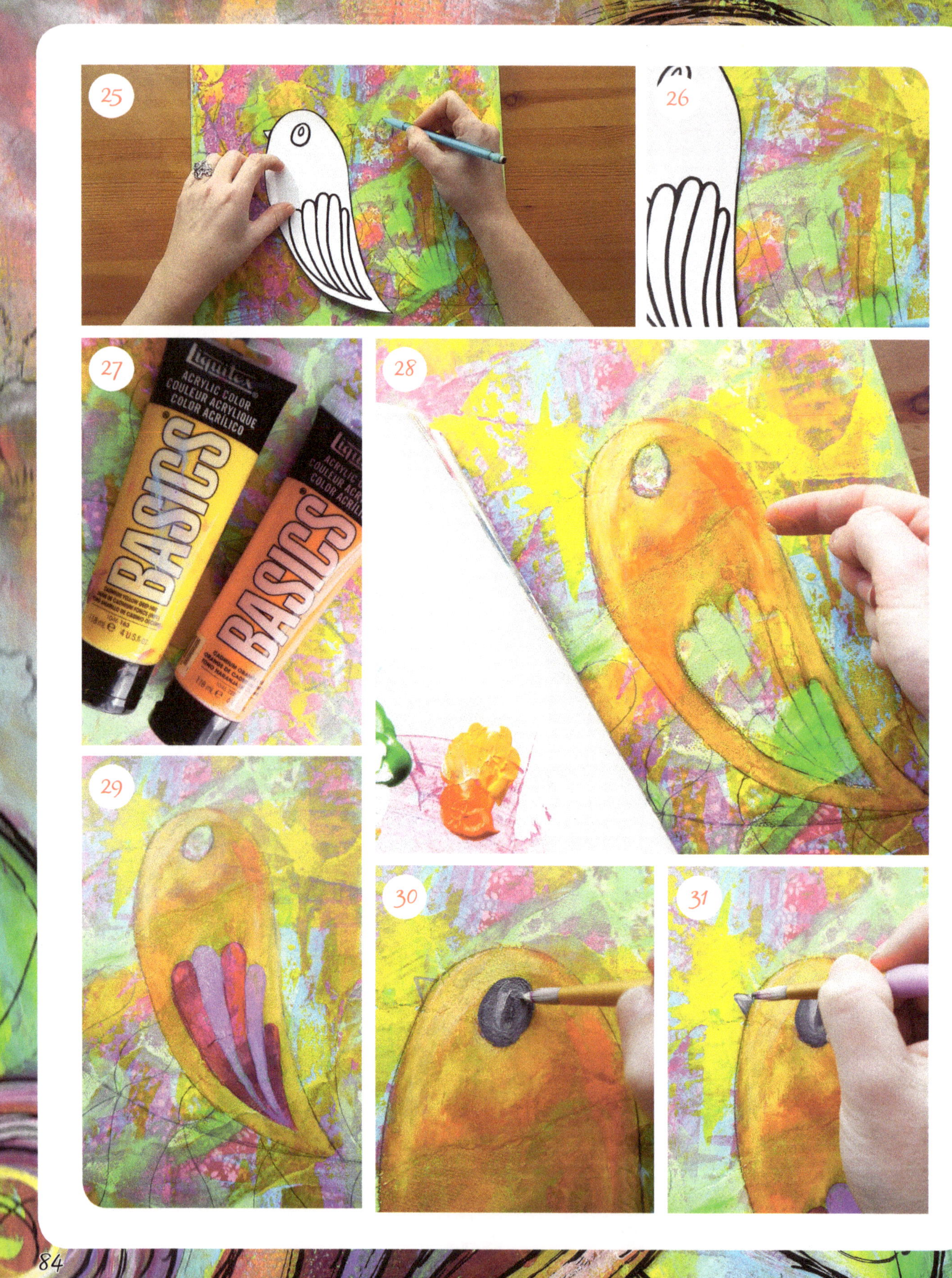

# A bird with style and personality

**25** Now is your chance to give your bird a little personality!
Use the template as a guide to draw his eye but, if you are game, then feel free to change the shape: you could make it round or more elongated, smaller or bigger, and place the pupil in a different spot (if you put it in the bottom left corner for instance, your bird will look shy or possibly worried!). Try coming up with different expressions!

**26** Do the same with the feathers: either use the template as reference or create your own (you could do just three feathers and make them smaller and more round for example).

**27** To stand out from the background a little but still complement the colours chosen earlier, let's use light and dark orange for the body of the bird (of course, feel free to choose different colours if you wish! He would also look great with shades of blue or pink).

**28** Dip your finger in light orange and fill in most of the body. While the paint is wet, add a few dark orange 'shadows'. Use white paint or gesso to create highlights (for example on the top left corner of the bird's head) but also if you want your paint to be more opaque. You can 'block' some of the design showing through from the collaged paper if you wish.

**29** Next, let's use a fine tip brush to fill in the feathers, starting with magenta for the first, third and fifth feather... And light purple for the rest.
I did not apply the paint too thick so I can still see a little bit of what's underneath.

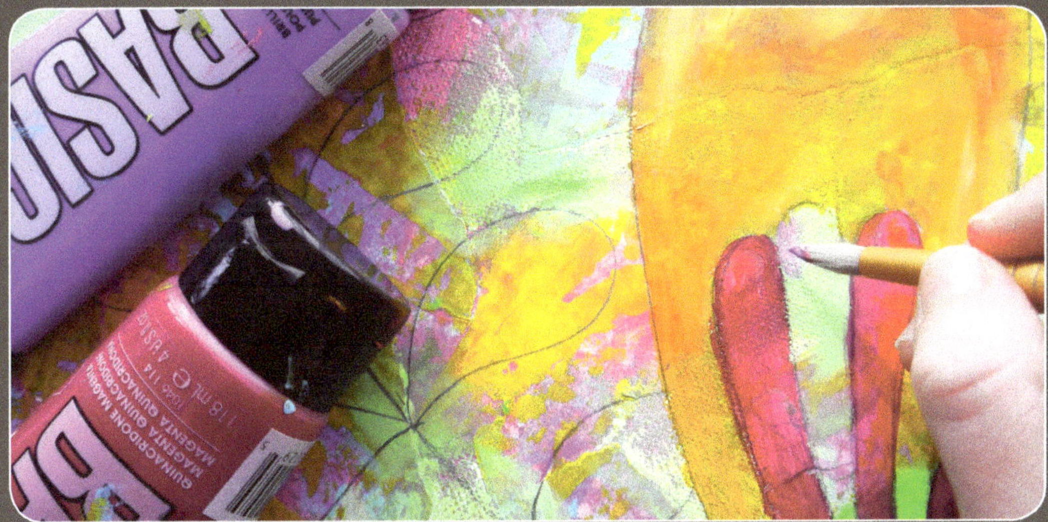

**30** Using your fine tip brush, paint the eye with dark grey paint and while it is still wet, add a little white and black to create some highlights and shadows. Don't worry about making it perfect for now, we can add more details later on.

**31** Now add a little dark grey to the beak, then a little white highlight on the top.

**32** By now I am sure you realise what great tools your fingers make!!
The leaves will look stunning with some 'Phtalo' or 'Viridian' green mixed with a little white.
The name may vary depending on the brand but the results will be very similar.
Use some of that gorgeous green (add some white or gesso to change the opacity and intensity) and alternate with the leftover apple green you mixed earlier.

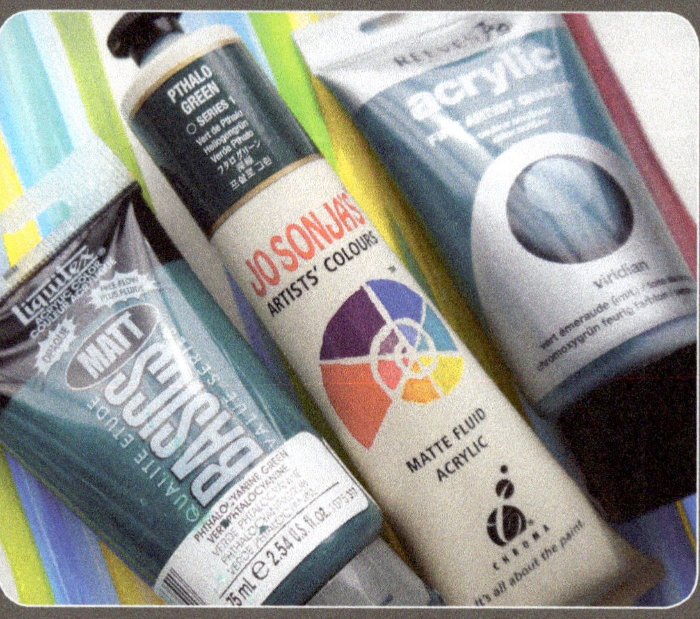

**33** Partially paint the leaves as we will be adding more colours very soon.
No need to do anything perfect here, just spread the paint with your finger without worrying too much about how it looks - just colour between the lines!

Then let everything dry... (You must be so sick of hearing me say that!!)

**34** Now, dip your finger into light blue/turquoise...

**35** ... And fill in the unpainted part of the leaves.
Again, add a little white here and there for variation and to make your leaves more opaque. This will help them stand out from the busy background. Let everything dry.

**36** Now let's create some highlights by adding a little yellow...
Vary the placement to create interest: on some leaves, add highlights on the top and on others, on the middle or bottom.

**37** Repeat but this time, with a little white. Keep the highlights subtle!
If for some reason you are not happy with what you have done then remember you can start again at any point - no big deal! Just let everything dry then cover all the leaves with gesso (don't worry if you go over the pencil lines). Then you can blend the colours once again, and add contrasting highlights.

**38** I felt like my leaves were a bit pale so I decided to add a bit of Phtalo/Viridian green for a little more pop. Keep adding colours until YOU are happy, it is your painting after all!

**39** There, happy now... :-)

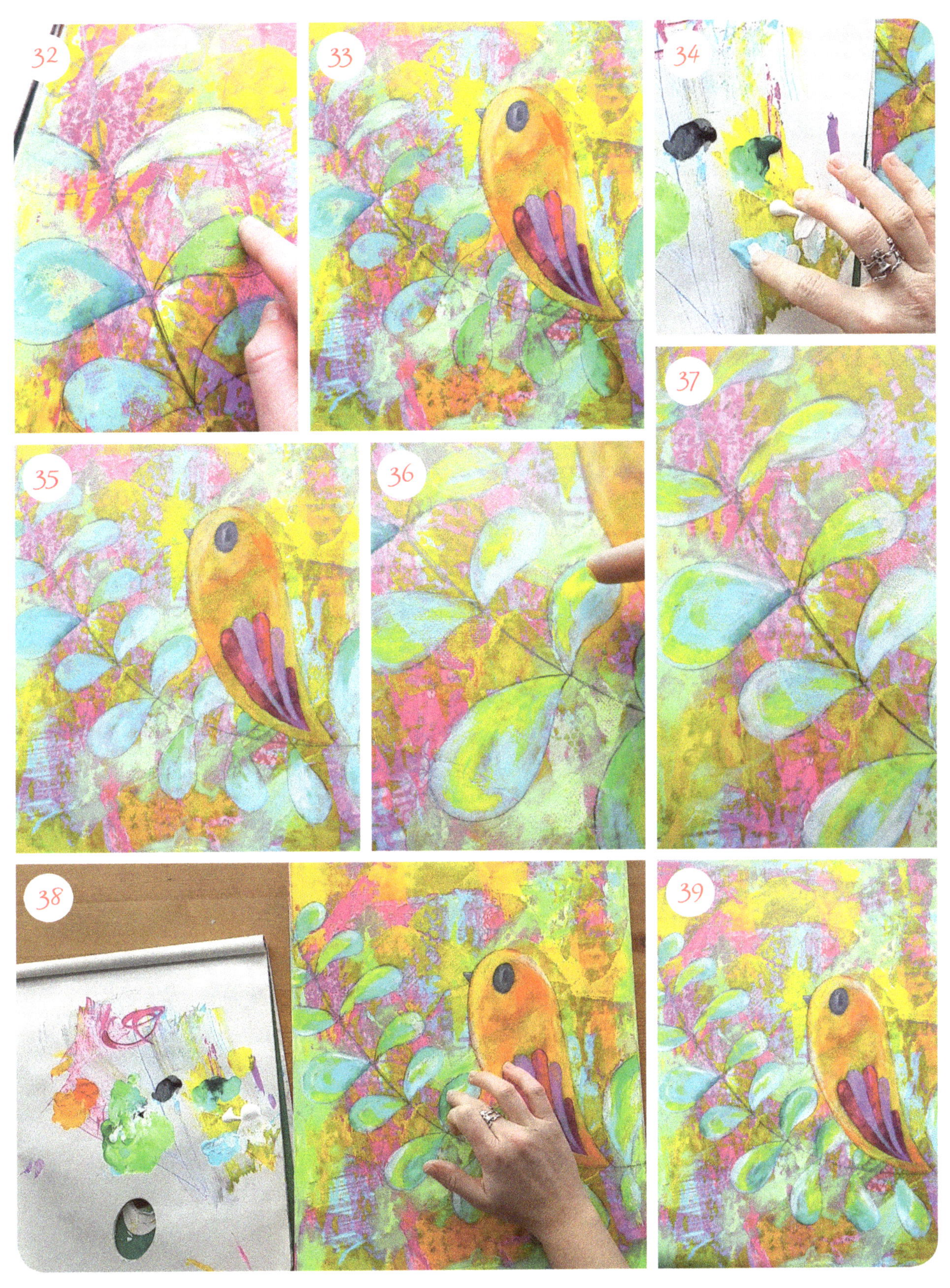


32
33
34
35
36
37
38
39

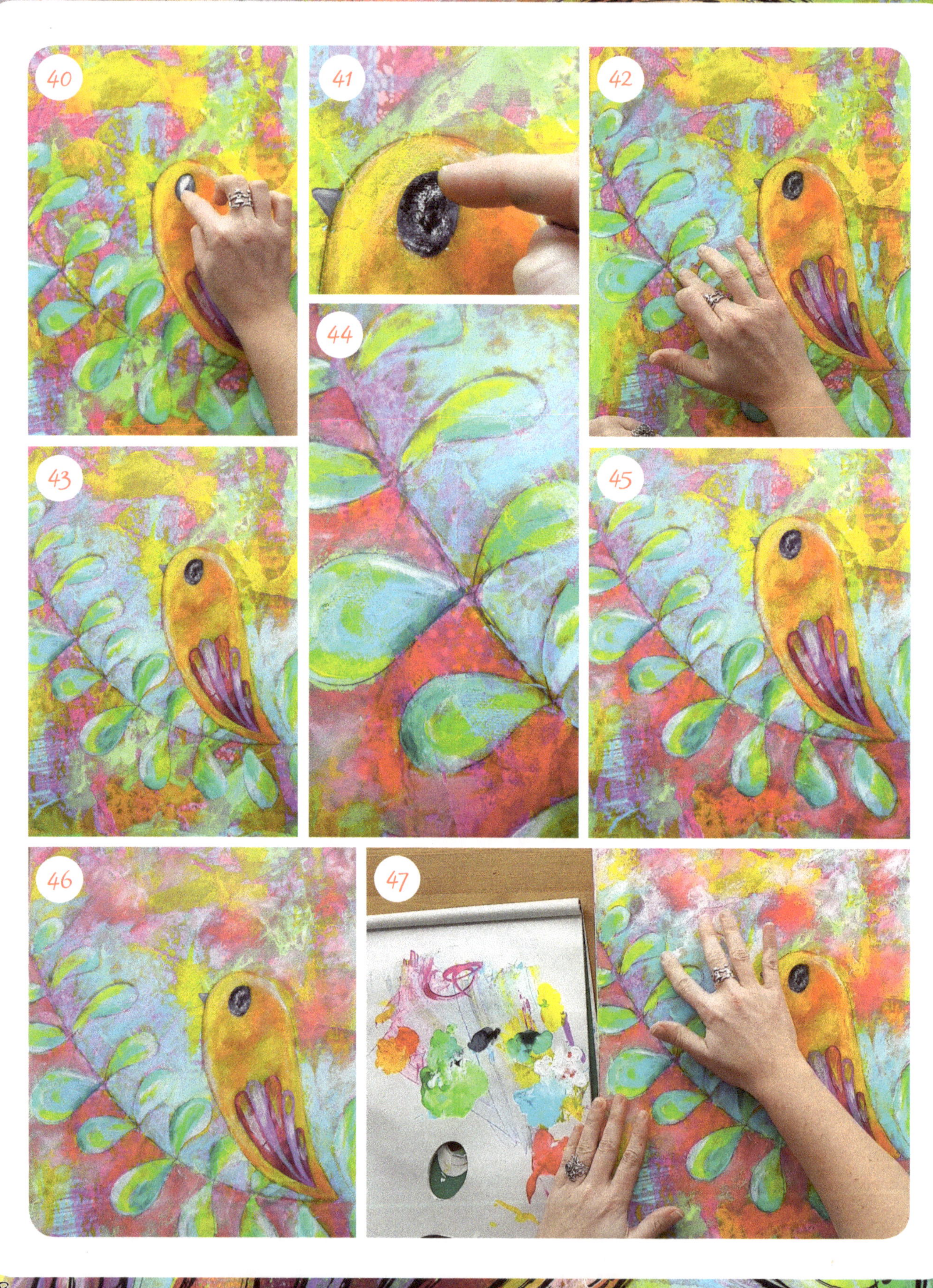

**40** While the leaves are drying, let's get back to the bird's feathers and eye...
Add subtle yellow and white highlights on the top of each feather (or choose any colour that will complement what you have).
On the eye, add a little white paint or gesso with your fingertip (or fine tip brush if you are painting a smaller bird), approximately from the top to the bottom, without touching the edges, to create the idea of light reflecting.

**41** Then dip your finger/brush in a little black paint and dab it on the left, and right, of the white you just added. Stand back to see if you are happy with it and if not, continue adding a little white and black until you are.

**42** Now stand back to assess how your leaves look against the background. If you look back at photo nb. 40, you may notice that the leaves don't stand out that much because the background looks busy. The easiest way to remedy this (and add fabulous interest in the process) is to add a layer of paint that will block out some of that 'busy-ness'!

First, dip your finger in a little light blue/turquoise and rub it all around the leaves and branch (the top part of the branch only). Add a little white every now and then to vary the intensity and opacity wherever you want to hide details. Paint a little away from your pencil lines in some areas to create a little gap for the background to show through.

**43** Make sure you also go around the bottom part of you bird as this will help him stand too!

**44** Now choose a contrasting colour for the bottom part of the branch. Here I am using Rose Pink by Jo Sonja (adding a little white to the Liquitex Primary Red will give you a similar colour). But you could also use the magenta from your background or mix your own colour. Never tell yourself you can't go on because you are missing one of the 'ingredients'!: use what you already own and create your own awesomeness!

> *" Improvising and finding alternatives is what makes us creative... And it gets easier with experience "*

**45** Just like you did with the blue, try to not always paint right against your pencil lines to leave a little gap. Now, didn't that make a huge difference? Compare this photo with nb. 39!

**46** To make your painting feel more uniform and balanced, it is important to repeat some elements throughout, such as shapes, texture or colour.

First, with the same colour you used on the bottom part of the branch, paint little patches here and there on your background (feel free to add a little white if the colour is too strong). Let dry.

**47** And then, to bring all the elements together, rub a little white paint or gesso on the whole painting: on the background (top and bottom), around the leaves and around the bird.

**48**   I would like to repeat an important concept: don't be too neat! I know it may not be obvious as a step on its own but, those little patches of colour you have been adding with your finger are part of the process of creating all that lovely texture and interest in your finished painting.

**49**   Remember to stand back every now and then to view the full picture...
Can you see how adding pink then white on the whole painting has brought everything together? Compare with photo nb. 43!
I chose white because it is a colour we have not used yet as a main element but you could try it with a different colour as well for a completely different feel...

## A pretty tail for a pretty bird

**50**   In our whimsical painting world, we can do whatever we like and that is such an amazing feeling! Dip your fine tip brush into the pink you used on the bottom part of the branch, and paint a simple spiral starting from the bottom of his body.

**51**   Repeat a few times, just to add a little 'fullness' to his tail. Let dry.

**52**   Now repeat with yellow, then white. Overlap the previous lines but don't follow them exactly so you can see the various colours showing through. Add a little white every now and then and make your lines blend into the body so the tail doesn't look 'disconnected'. Let dry.

**53**   Repeat the process one last time with magenta, then add a few white highlights.

**54**   For extra interest, add a little white paint or gesso on your finger and rub it along his belly, and a little on the top of his head/back. No harsh lines, keep it soft...
You can also add a few very thin soft white lines on his 'cheek'.

## The finishing touches...

**55**   When all the elements of a painting have soft edges and nothing stands out too much, it is incredible how strengthening and darkening a few lines can make a huge difference. You will soon see what I mean!
Gently trace the outline of your bird (body, eye and beak) with a fine tip marker (0.7 mm or similar). You could also do this with an extra fine tip brush dipped in fluid black paint or black ink (the lines will be a little thicker). If you are unsure which one will give you the best result and control, practice first on a piece of scrap paper or on your palette.

*" It always amazes me to see how a simple black line can create such a huge pop in any painting! "*

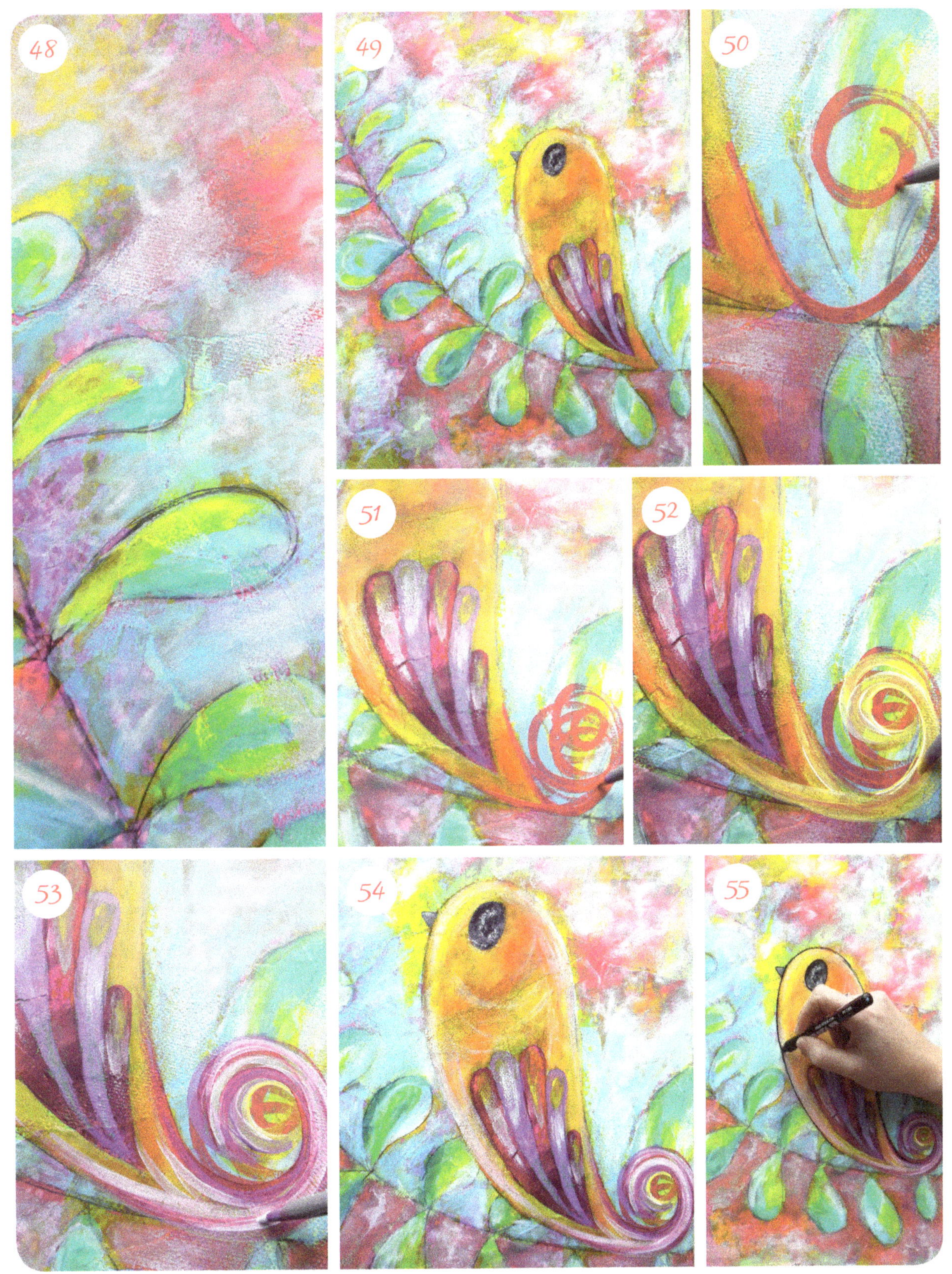


48
49
50
51
52
53
54
55

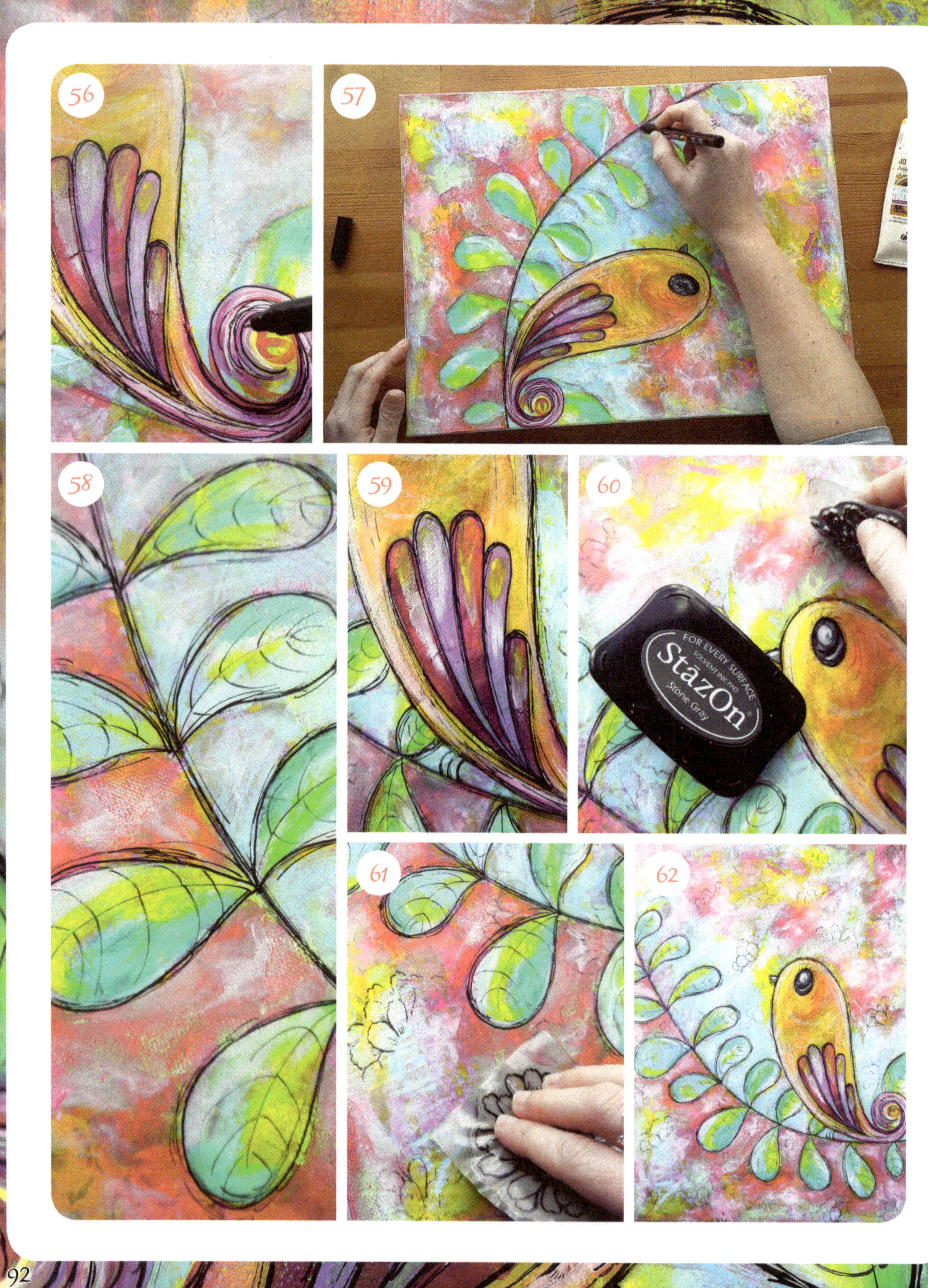


56
57
58
59
60
StazOn
FOR EVERY SURFACE
SOLVENT INK PAD
Stone Gray
61
62

**56** You can give the outlines of the leaves a 'sketched' feel by going over your strokes a few times (around the body, feathers and tail as well). If you would prefer a neater look, then just go over each outline once - but seriously, after all this work to loosen you up? :-)

**57** Repeat on the branch (rotating your surface makes things a lot easier sometimes!)...

**58** ... And around each leaf. Then add a few loose lines in the middle of each one for 'veins'.

**59** How has your bird been standing upright all this time without feet? He has been putting on a great balancing act so be kind to him, draw three little curved lines to help him out!

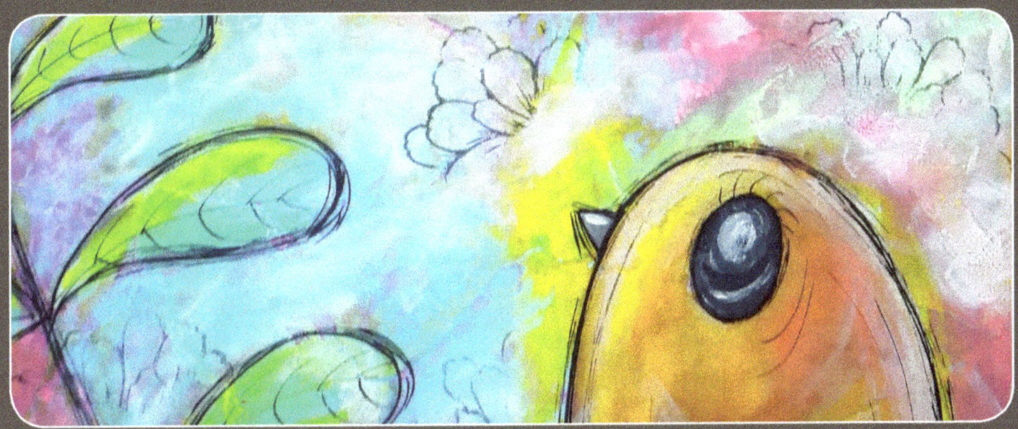

## Using a stamp to bring unity to your painting

Remember when I said that repeating elements throughout a painting helps bring everything together? You did this using colour earlier (with pink and white), now let's do it with pattern!

**60** Grab an inkpad and a stamp of your choice. The actual pattern of the stamp doesn't matter that much because we just want part of it to show to create 'abstract' texture. I would just avoid anything with a chunky/heavy design - and, if you must know, I am using the Stampendous 'Zinnia' stamp here - really gorgeous!

I also recommend using Stazon inkpads from Tsukineko because I know they allow you to stamp on anything and dry quickly. To add contrast, use a darker shade (such as this 'Stone Gray' which is a little softer than black).

**61** Press your stamp onto the inkpad then on your background. Either ink the whole stamp and bend it a little to only stamp part of the design, or simply only ink part of the design then stamp. The idea behind this is that the stamped area should not be the main focus on the painting! Make sure you rotate the stamp so each print isn't exactly the same.

**62** And finally... YOU. ARE. DONE!! Give yourself a hug and enjoy your gorgeous new friend!

*The finished painting is showcased on page 103*

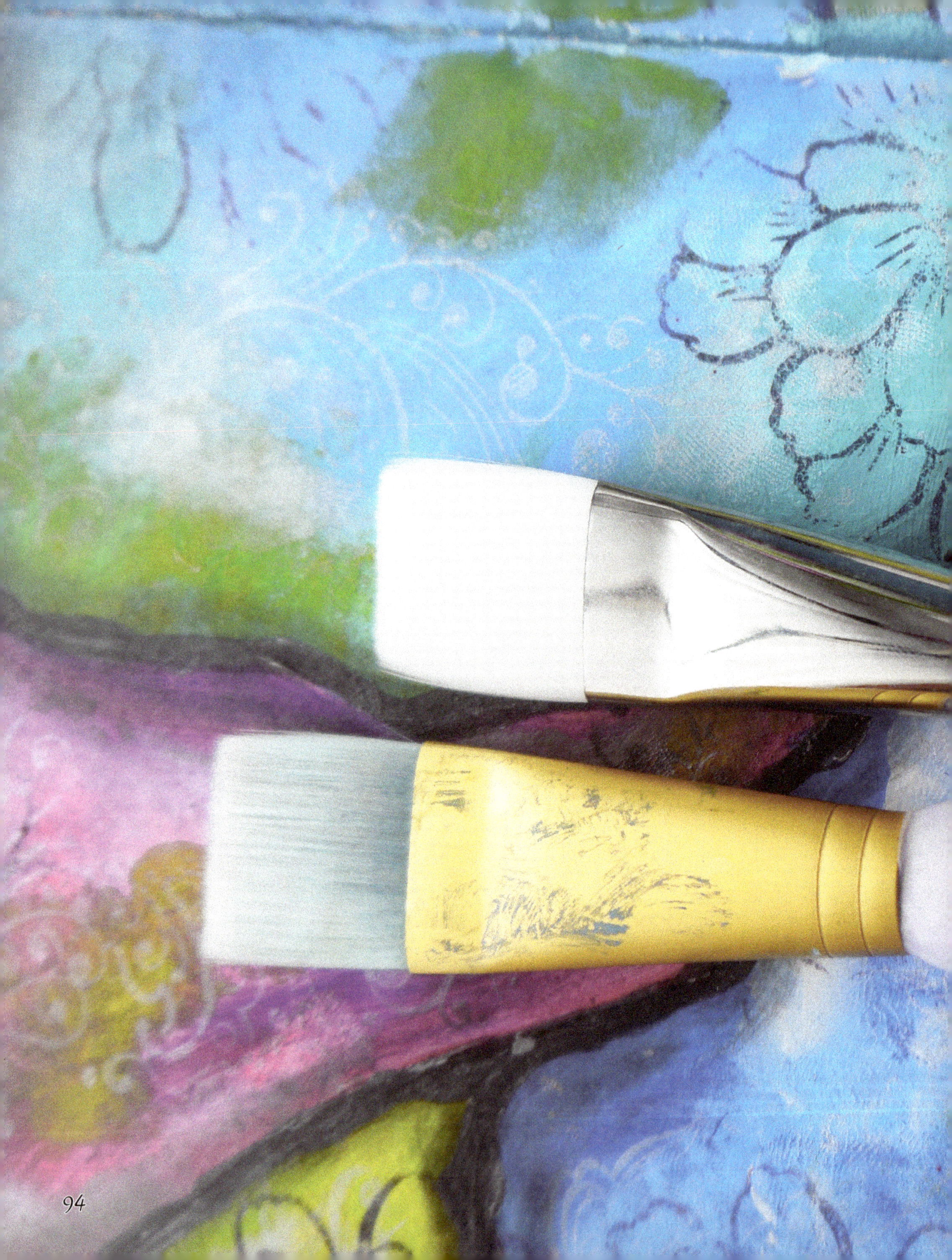

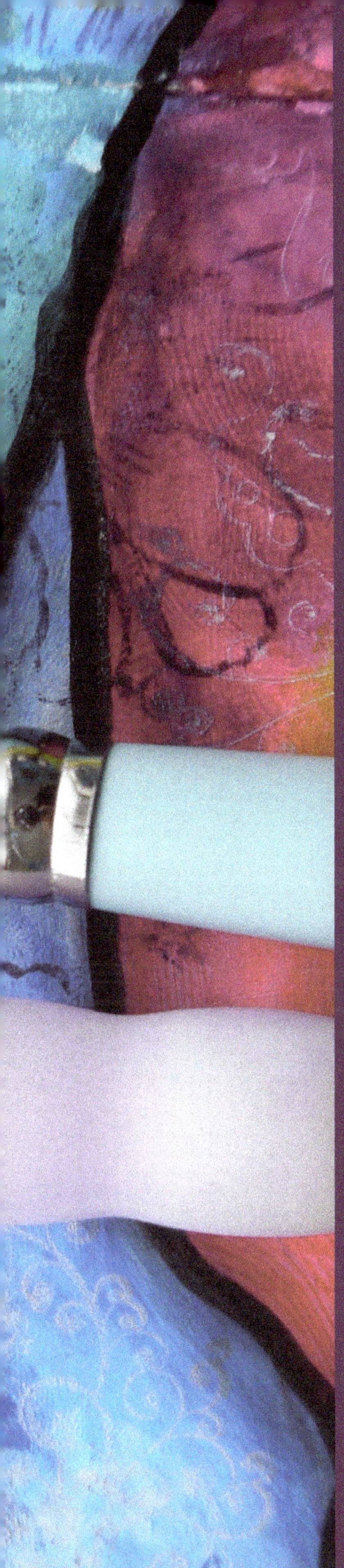

# Inspiration Gallery

### Wow, what a journey!

You have painted, stamped, 'gesso-ed', drawn, stencilled and got your hands dirty...

You have learnt how to...
• Create easy and powerful backgrounds,
• Add texture with paint, stamps, modelling paste,
• Create a focal point and an abstract piece,
• Mix colours, change their intensity and opacity,
• Use stencils with various mediums,
• Create shadows and borders with a gelato sticks...
And so much more!

You have played, experimented, made mistakes, corrected them, built your confidence and created art that made you feel happy!

### So, what next?

Don't stop!!!!!!!!!!
Apply what you have just learnt, in your own way!

Choose different stencils, stamps or make your own...
Choose a new focal point, vary the placement...
Try different colour combinations...
Experiment on different surfaces: paper, cardboard...
Don't think too much, just keep going!

In this section, I included a few examples of other paintings I created to show you what varied and wonderful results you can get, using similar techniques and art supplies as in the chapters of this book. I hope they will be a source of inspiration to keep you motivated!

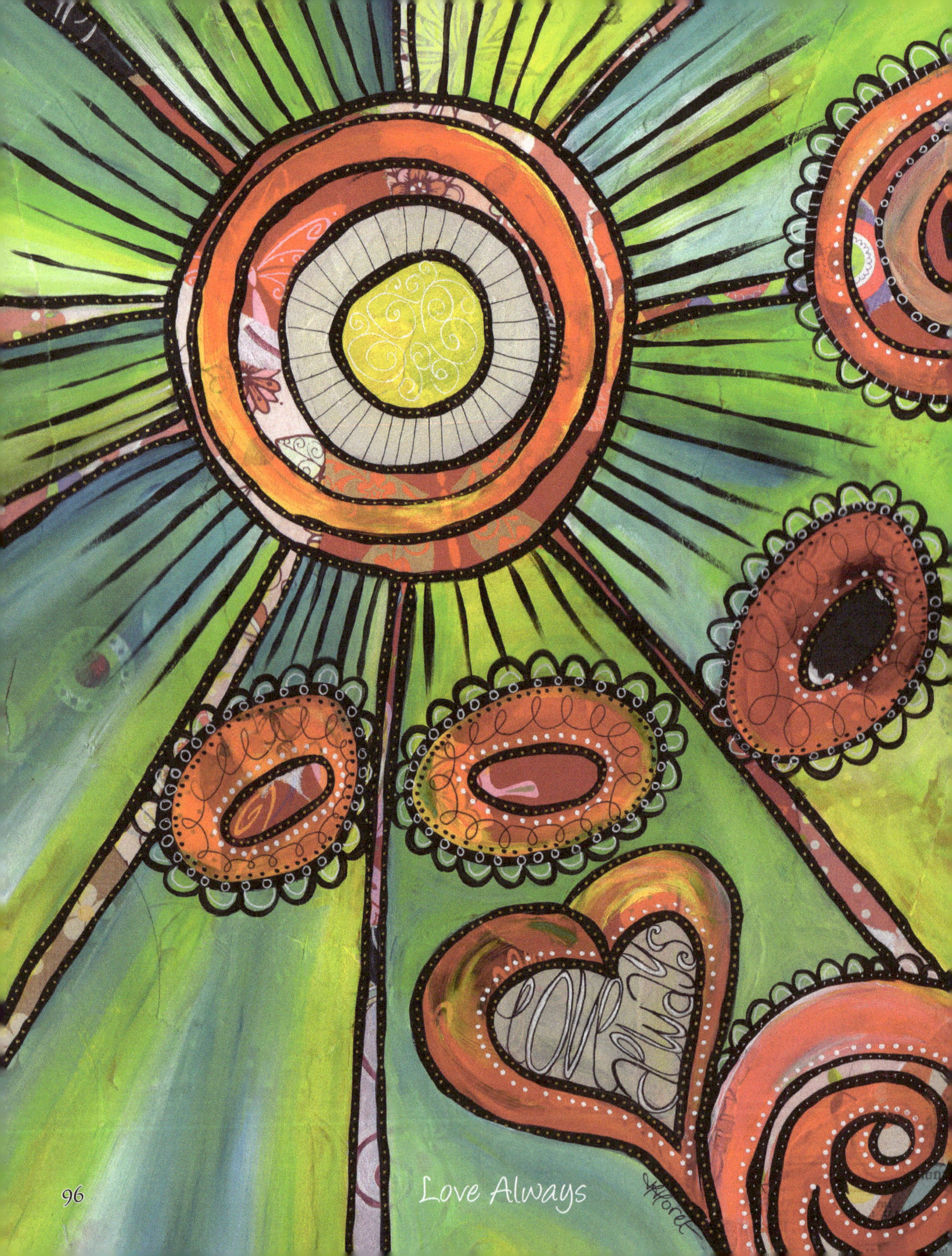
Love Always

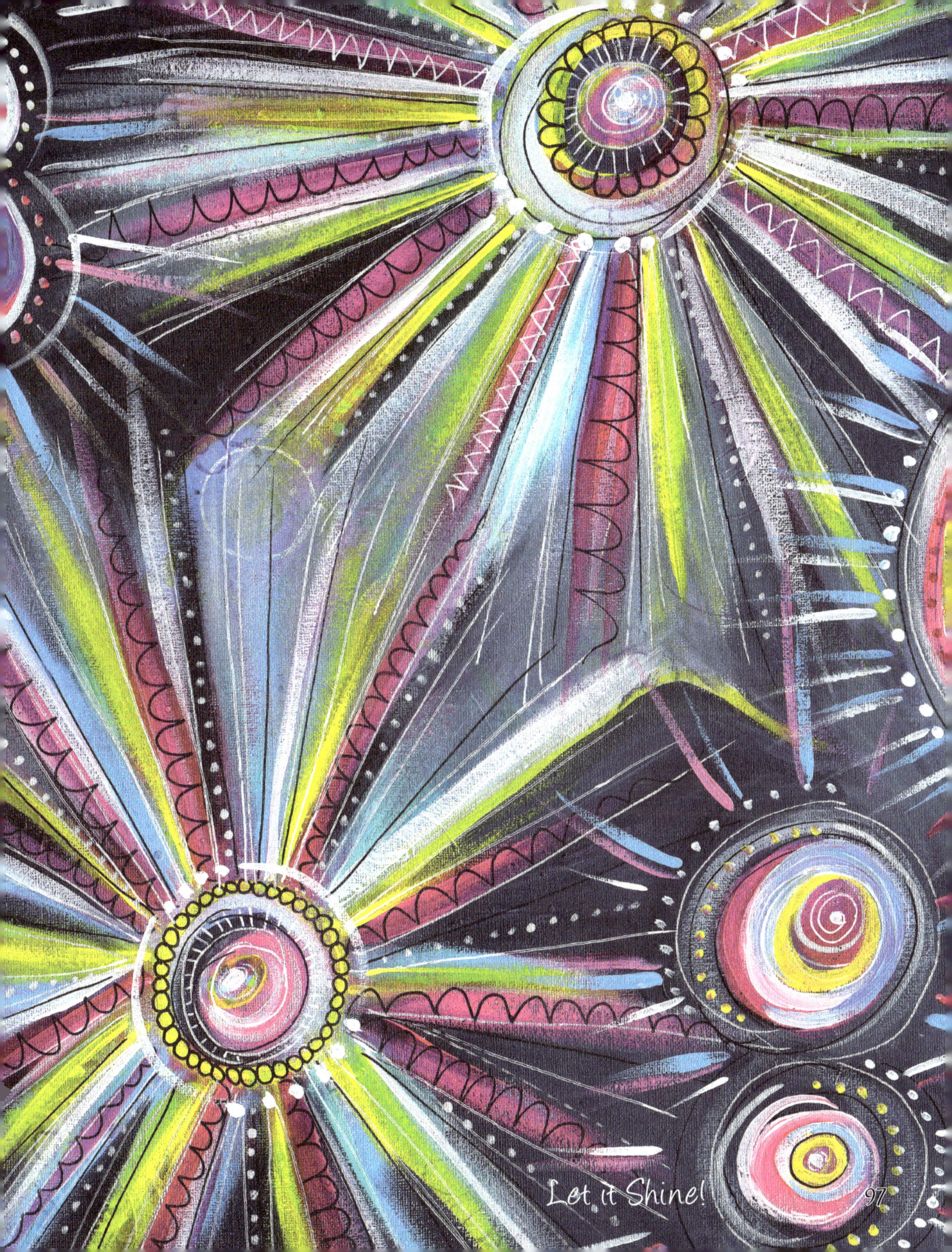
Let it Shine!

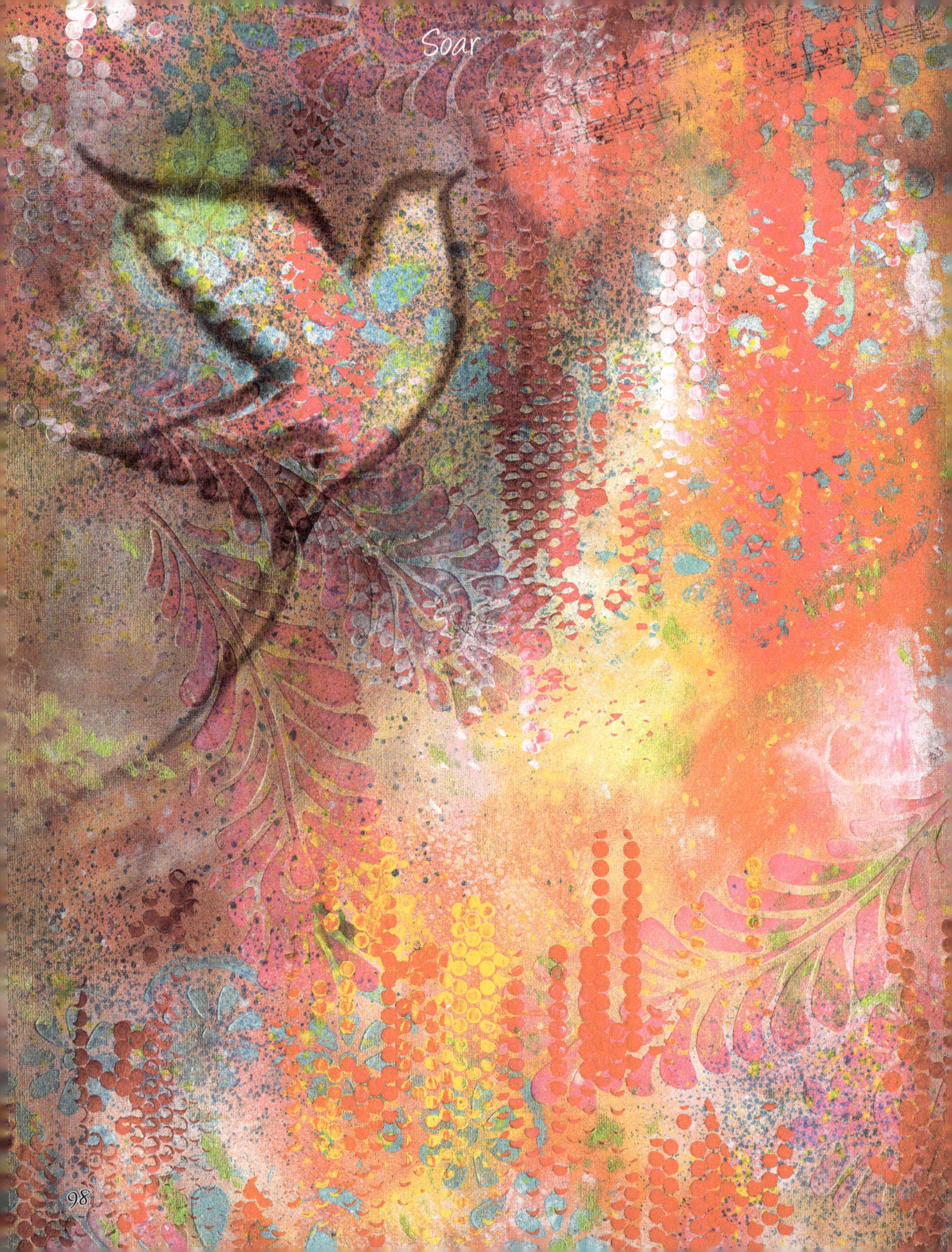
Soar

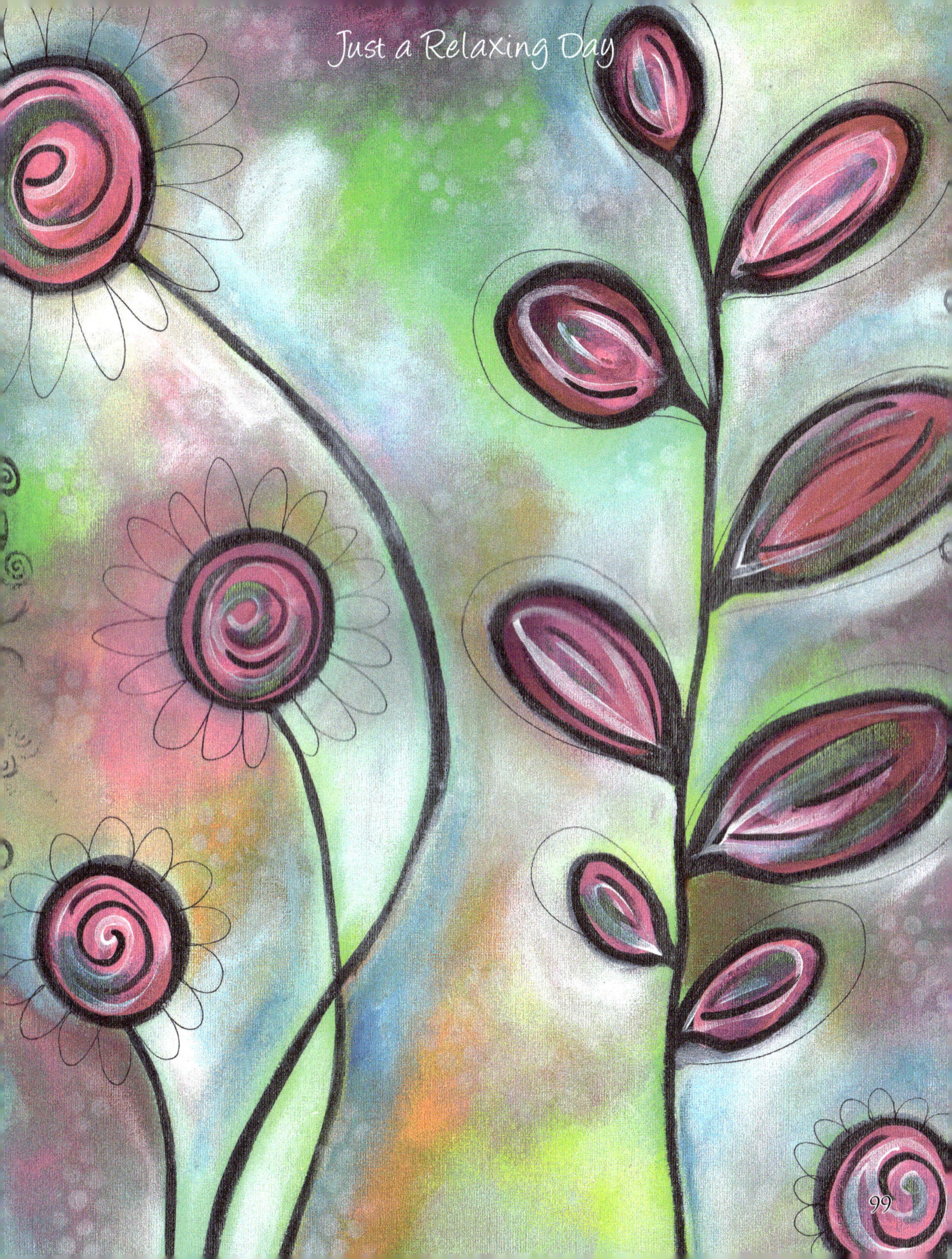
Just a Relaxing Day

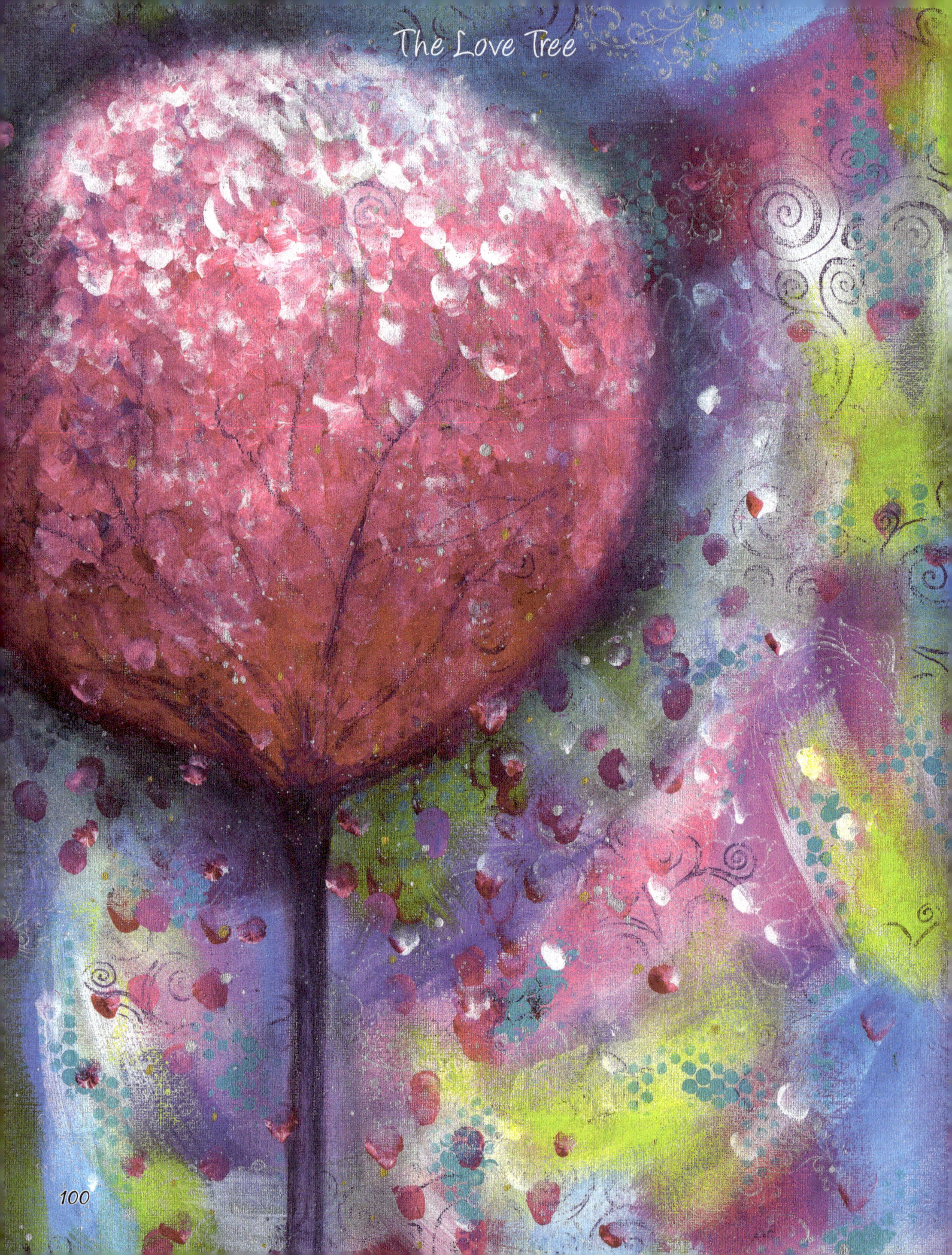

The Love Tree

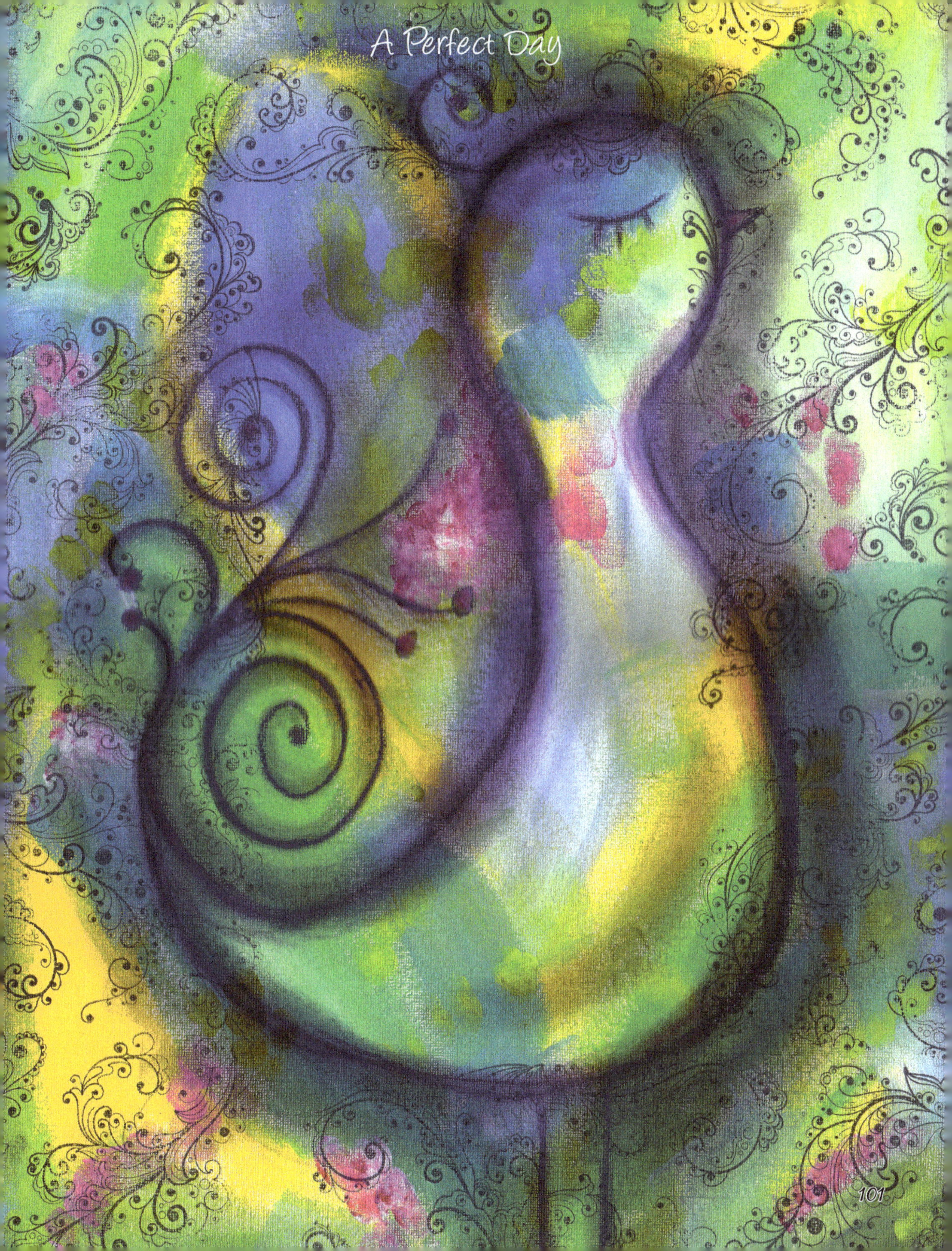

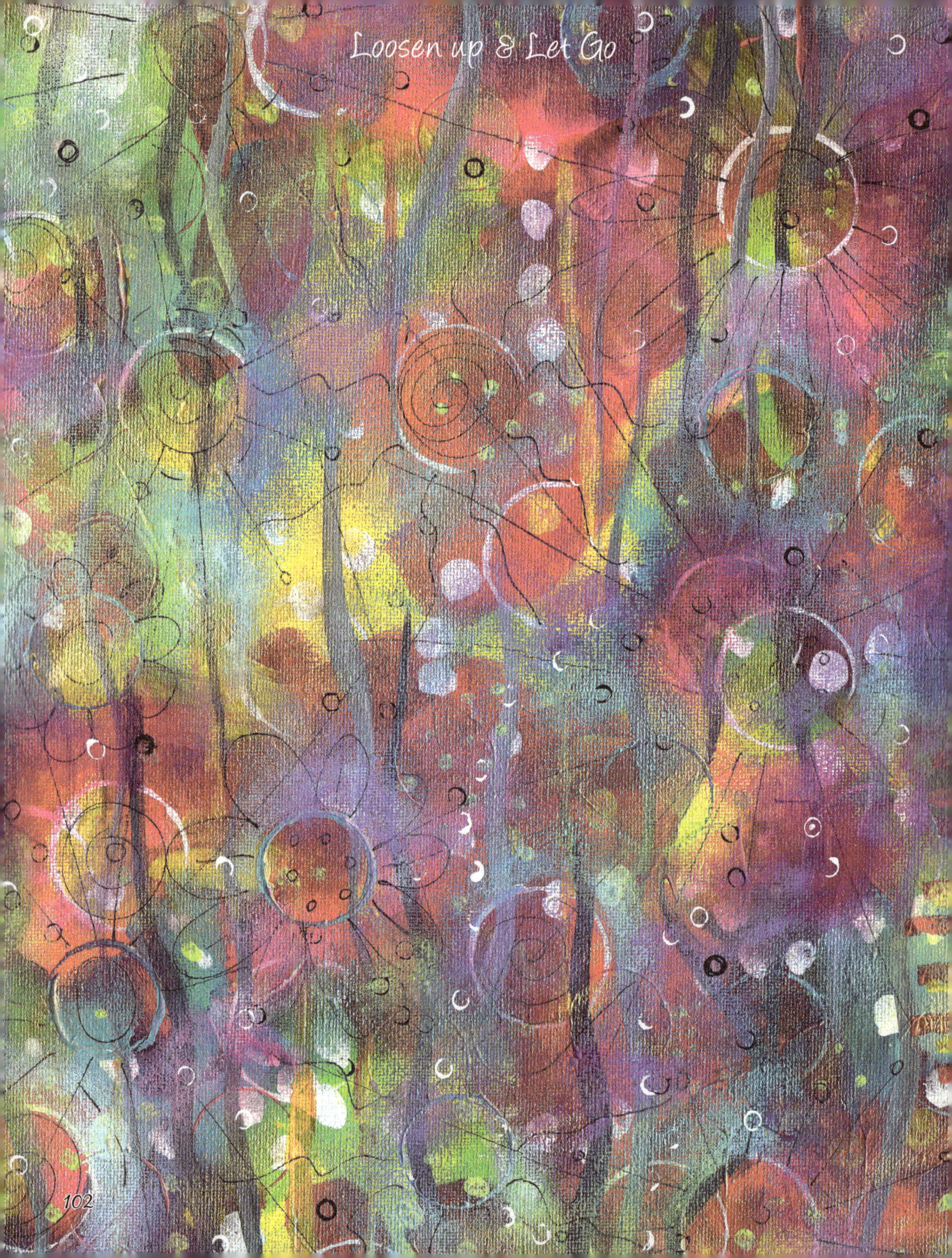
Loosen up & Let Go

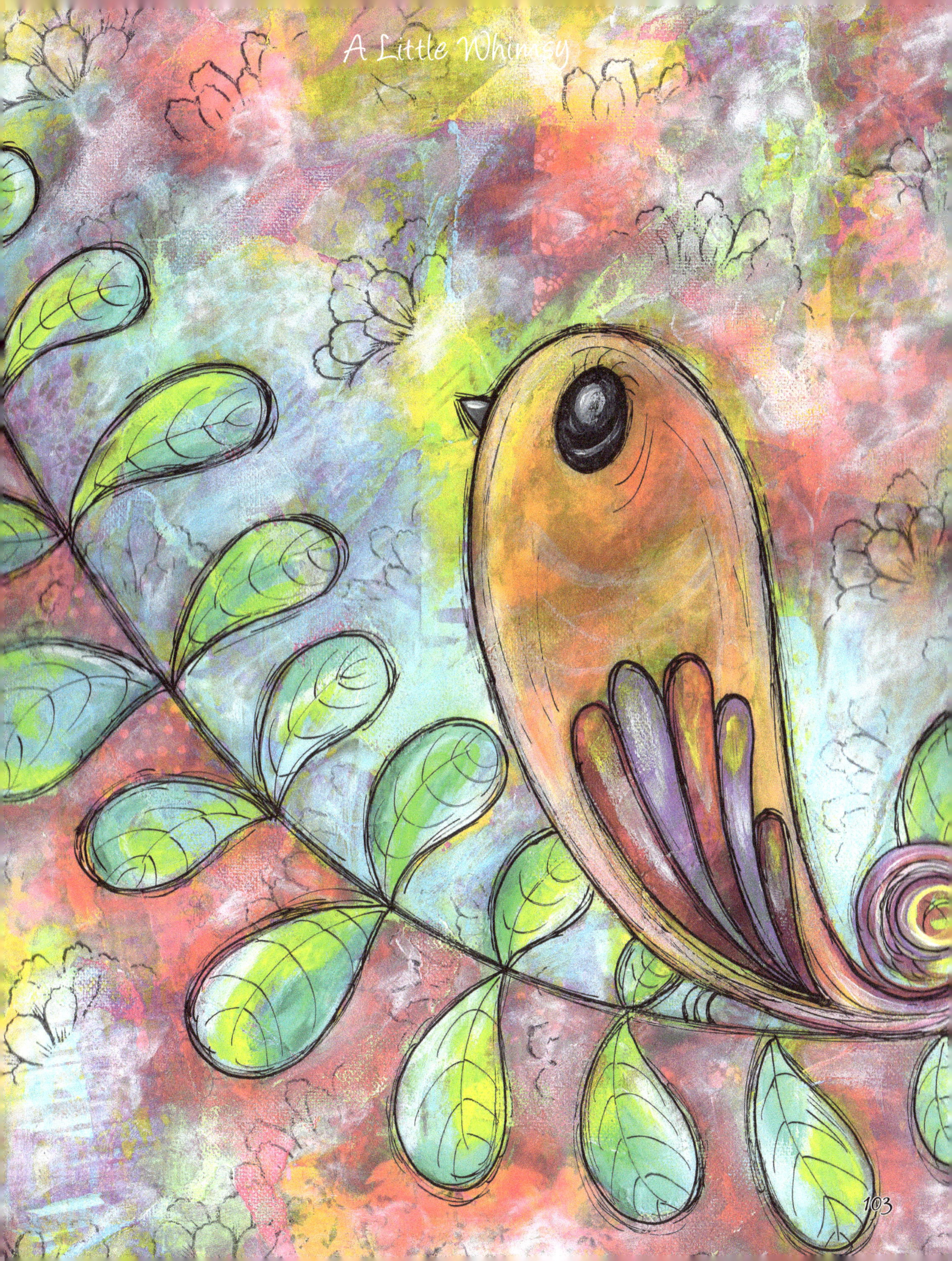
A Little Whimsy

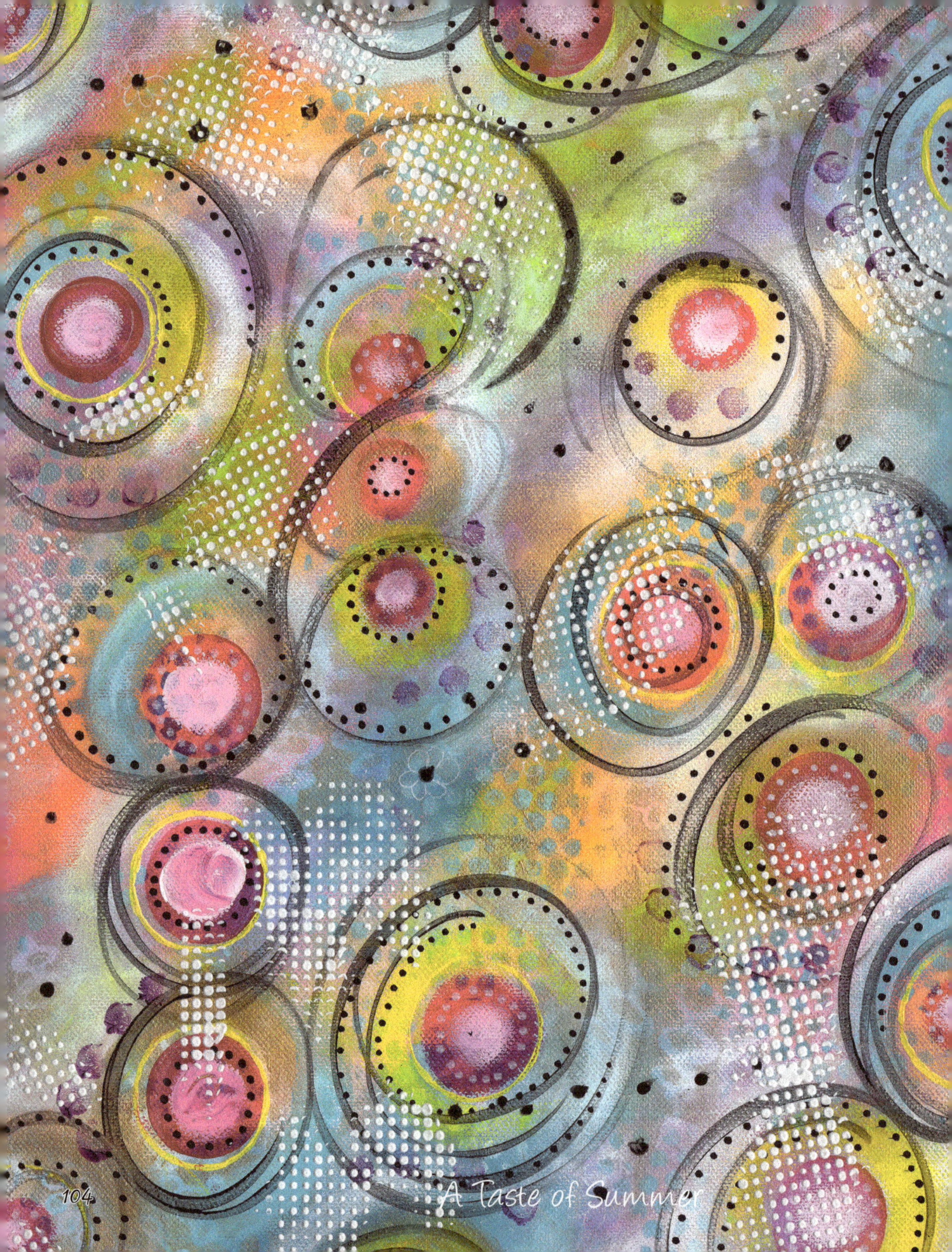



A Taste of Summer

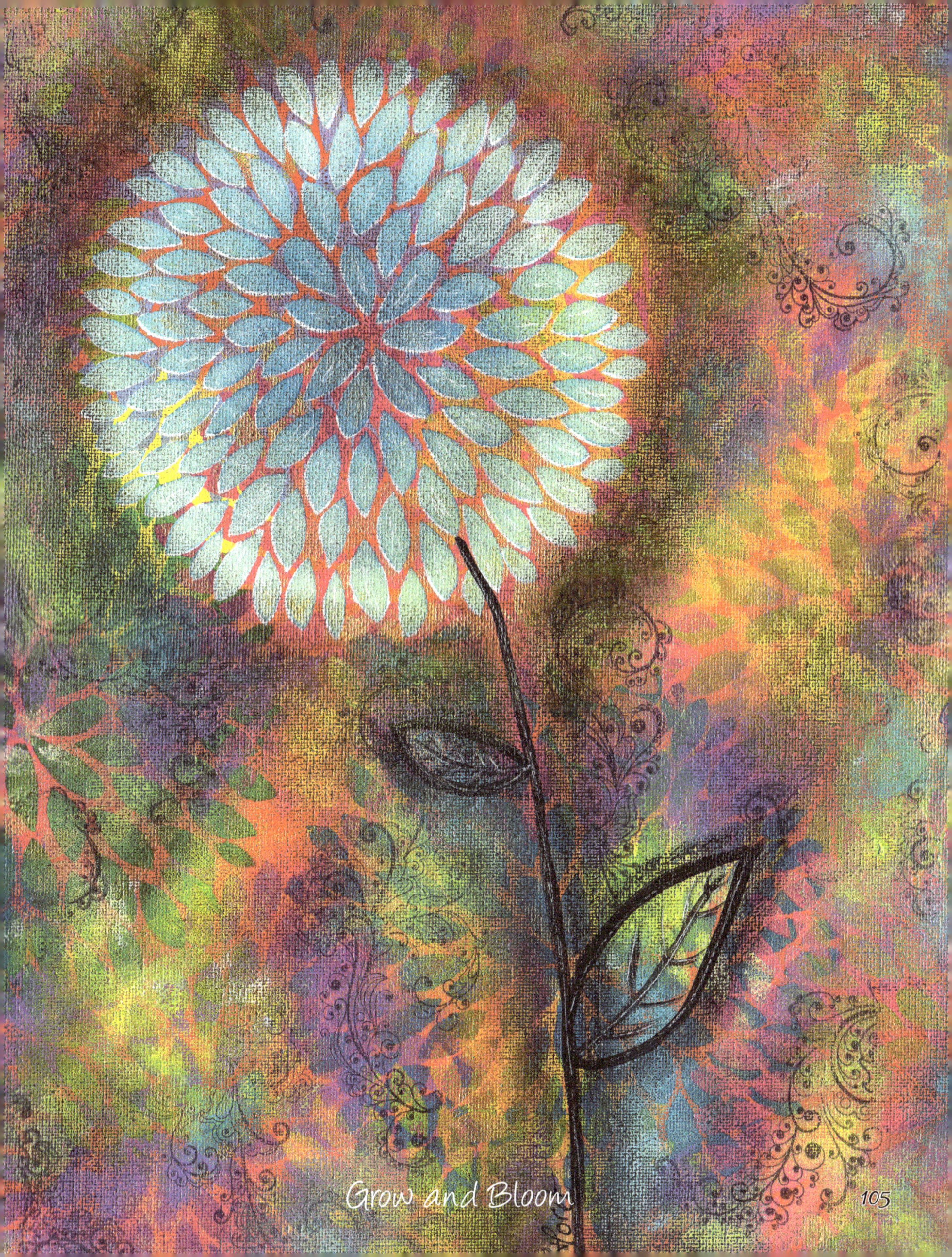

Grow and Bloom

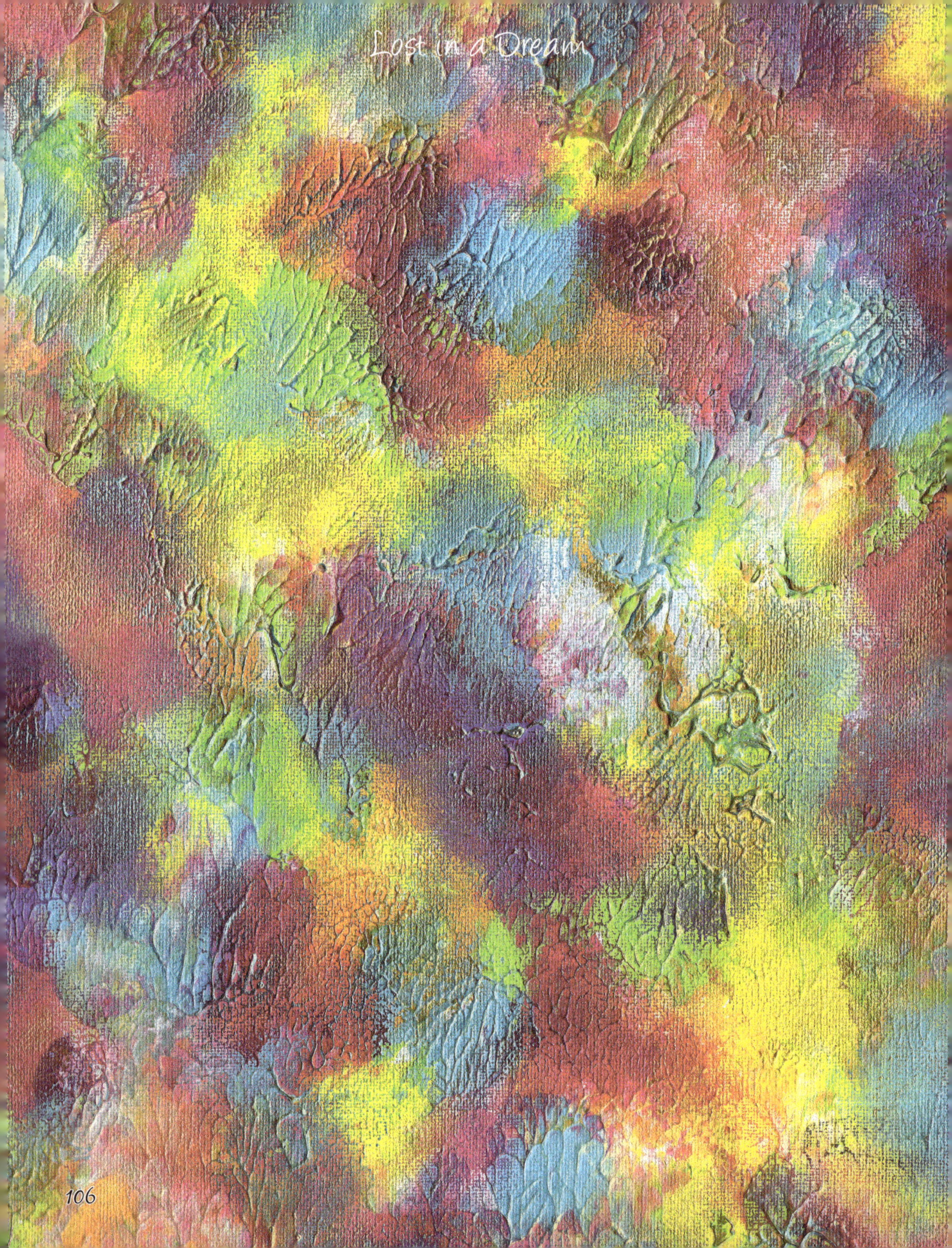
Lost in a Dream

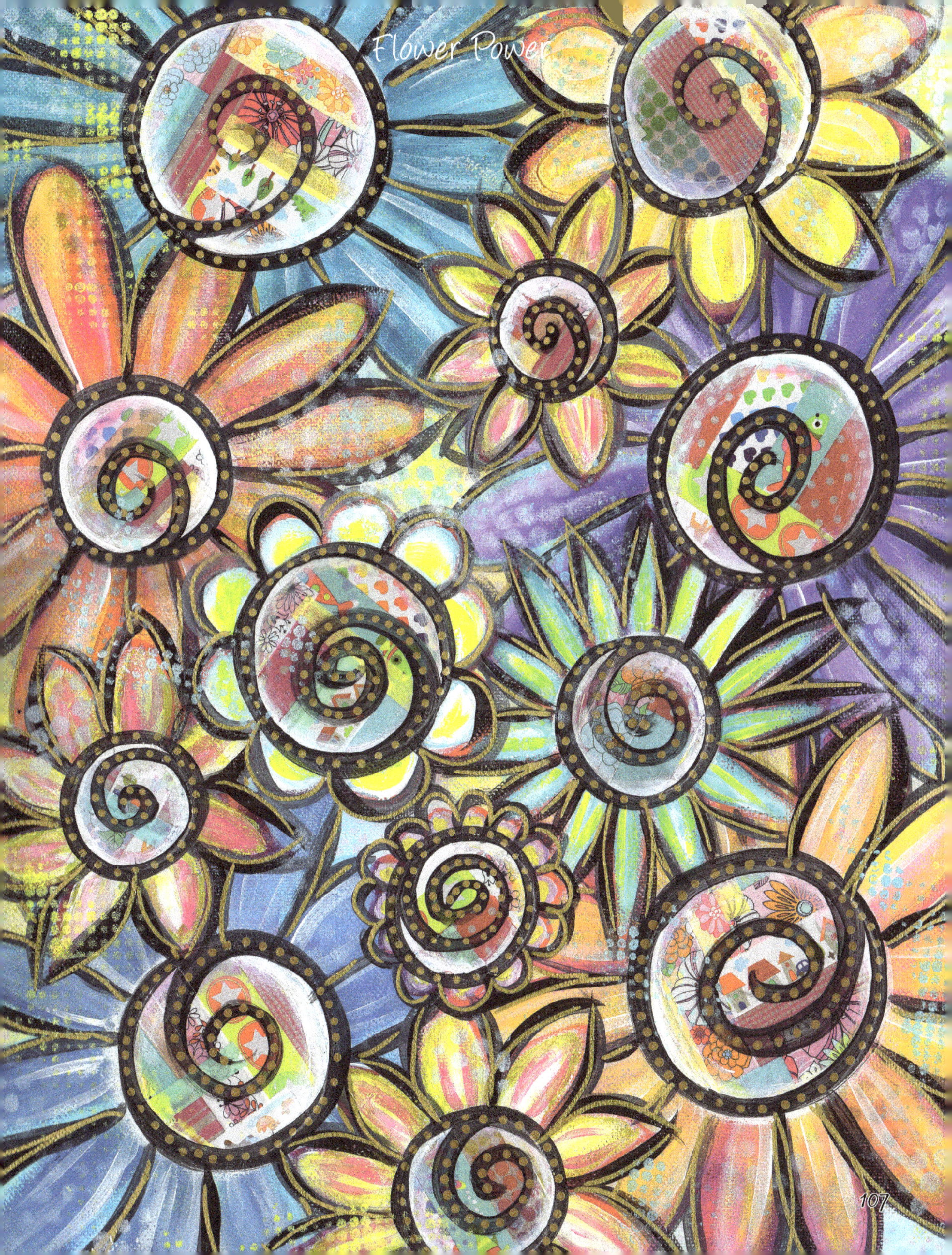
Flower Power

# Questions, comments?

## The Creative Tribe

If you would like to ask me a question about the book, share a photo of the work you created from these tutorials (I would absolutely love to see what you did!) or simply send me some loving feedback (or suggestions on how to improve this book) then leave me a comment:

### mimibondi.com/the-creative-tribe

## Find me on social media!

**Facebook**
For a little bit of everything: work in progress, new paintings and videos, new posts and exhibitions, find me on Facebook: facebook.com/mimibondiart

**Instagram**
For (almost) daily posts about other highly talented & inspiring artists, photos of my work in progress, art journal pages and a few snippets from my personal life, find me on Instagram: instagram.com/mimibondi

**YouTube**
Free mixed media tutorials taken from my art journals and anything that just works best as a video: youtube.com/mimibondi

**Pinterest**
Pinterest is an amazing social media platform where I collect TONS of ideas and inspiration on various art boards such as 'For the Love of Mixed Media', 'The Beauty of Abstract Art', 'Whimsical Birds, 'Whimsical Girls', 'Inspiring Words' and much more: pinterest.com/mimibondi

## Sunshine Newsletter

Now that we have found each other, I hope we can stay connected!

**My Sunshine Newsletter is all about positivity and the BEST
way to keep up with all the good stuff in one central place:**

• *Be the first to know about new books and online workshops*

Who knows what I have in store for you lovely artists! But when new goodies are
cooking, I will be sharing them with you in my newsletter and give you priority access!

• *Find out about new paintings I create*

I will share new artworks with you and hopefully provide you with a little inspiration!

• *Think positive, Be Positive, Act Positive*

I am all about positivity and love to find, write and share articles and tools that can
make a positive impact in your life...

• *Free art journal video tutorials*

If you want to learn new techniques and follow me along while I chat, play and
experiment in my art journal, you will find video links to my tutorials in the newsletter!

• *Inspiring talented artists*

Whenever I come across artists who blow my mind, I think they deserve a shout out
so I do my bit by writing a post about them or sharing a link to their website so you
too can be amazed and inspired!

**My Sunshine Newsletter comes out about once a month and if
you are not receiving it yet, visit this page now before you forget!**

# mimibondi.com/newsletter

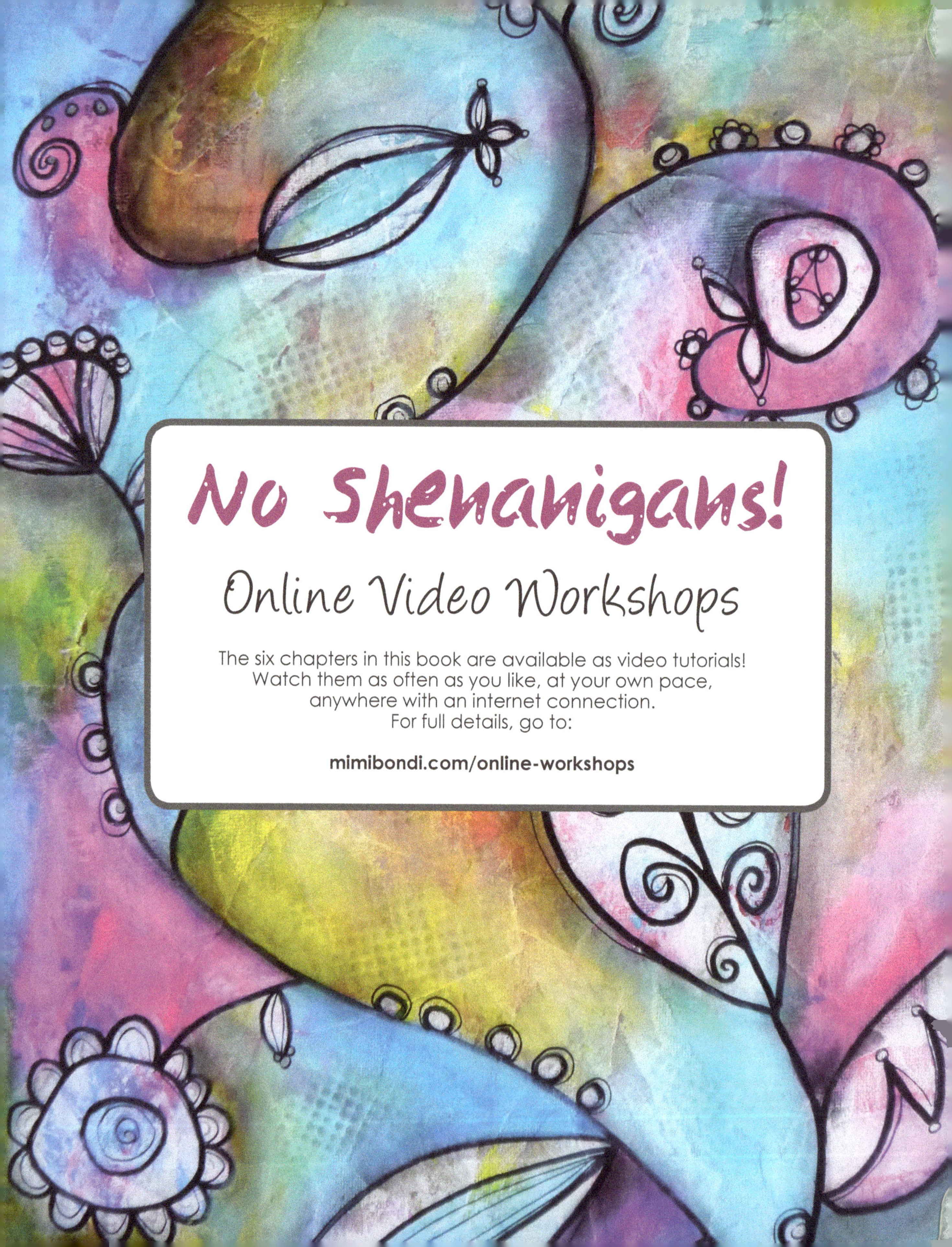
No Shenanigans!
Online Video Workshops

The six chapters in this book are available as video tutorials!
Watch them as often as you like, at your own pace,
anywhere with an internet connection.
For full details, go to:

mimibondi.com/online-workshops

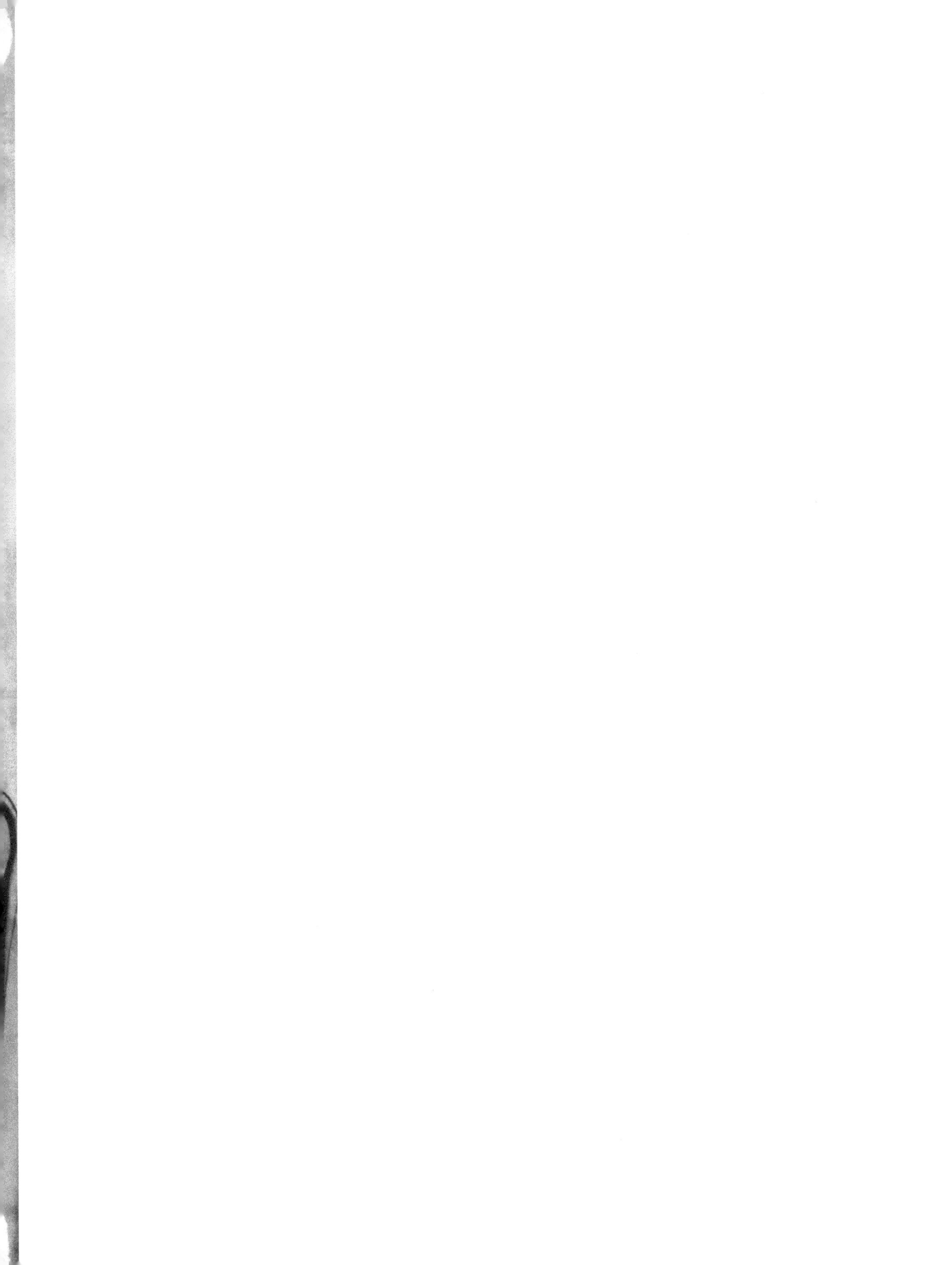